"Bali Feeds Your Dreams"

Photography
Fabrizio Bellardetti
all photos copyrighted

Smaller photos
Dale Bertrand
all photos copyrighted

Writing, Book Design,
Selection of Famous Quotes
Della Burford

Azatlan Publishing
ISBN 978-1-927825-05-1

Bali Feeds Your Dreams

Part 1 Living the Dream

I Made Sidia in Bali is Art Director of Sangga Paripurna - a Dance Company who are living their dreams. The mentor of the Dance Company is I Made Sidia and I Made Sijia as the tradition of dance and puppetry is passed down from generation to generation. Many members of the family are involved including his wife WayanSwastini, son Sugi and their daughter and cousins. It is a family effort Many of the hundreds of students learn dance from when they are small children and some later become professional performers.

Part 2 Sharing my Dreams

Della Burford created a Dream Wheel every year for 40 years and on them recorded her most important dreams. Many dreams were manifested into books, performances and paintings and shared internationally. Dale Bertrand helped in many aspects of the dream work. The painting of "Dream Wheels" amd Dream Keys" were both shown in Bali at Karja's Studio in a collaborative show swith Wayan Karja. Many friends attending including those below in 2016.

Part 3 Making the Dream

Many friends came to be part of the Spirit of Writing and Art and made this dream come true so thank you. Thanks to Fabrizio Belardetti for photography, and to Norah Burford for Coordinating, and Karja for sharing his villa/studio and mentoring. Thanks Dale Bertrand for sharing Medicine Wheels and photos. Sylke Gande for Sacred Art, Ayden Graham for music, Leema Graham for dance, & Charlyne Chiasson for Feng Shui. Thanks to Grace Po and Wallace Murray for joining painting and also Saharnaz Fara for a yoga class. Also Eric Bobrow, Holly Yurxa and Warren Burford for joining in .Thanks Dewa, Wayan & Nyoman, and Ketut .Big thanks to Michelle Pettit for arranging Pelanghi School and Ketut and Christina Hatala at Ahmed. Thanks to everyone at Santra Putra including Puta. If I have forgotten someone sorry as there are many to thank so thank you all.

Bali feeds your dreams!

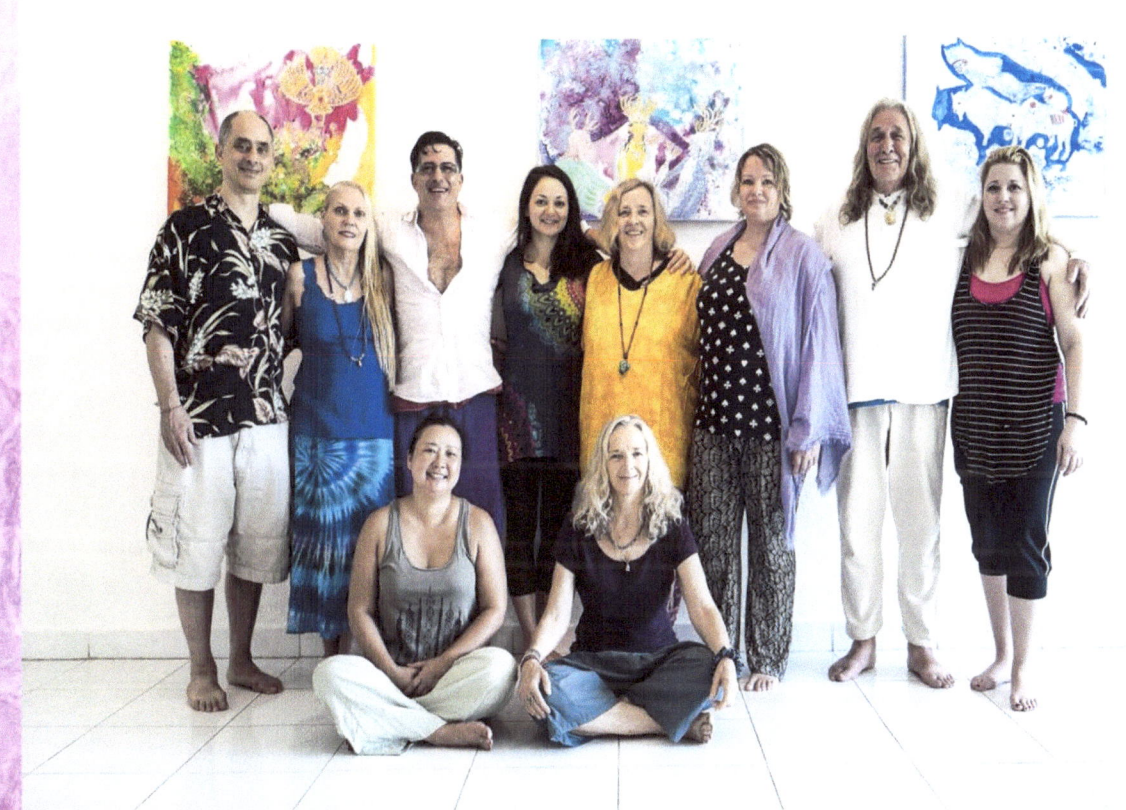

Living the Dream

I Made Sidia in Bali is Art Director of Sangga Paripurna
– a dance company who are living their dreams. The dance company is mentored by I Made Sidia and Sijia as the tradition is to pass talent down in the family from generation to generation. Many members of the family are involved including I Made Sidia's wife Wayan Swastini, son Sugi and daughter and cousins. It is a family effort. Many of the students of the Dance Compnay learn dance from when being small children and some are now professional performers.

"Keep your dreams alive. Understand to achieve anything requires faith and belief in yourself, vision, hard work, determination, and dedication. Remember all things are possible for those who believe."
Gail Devers

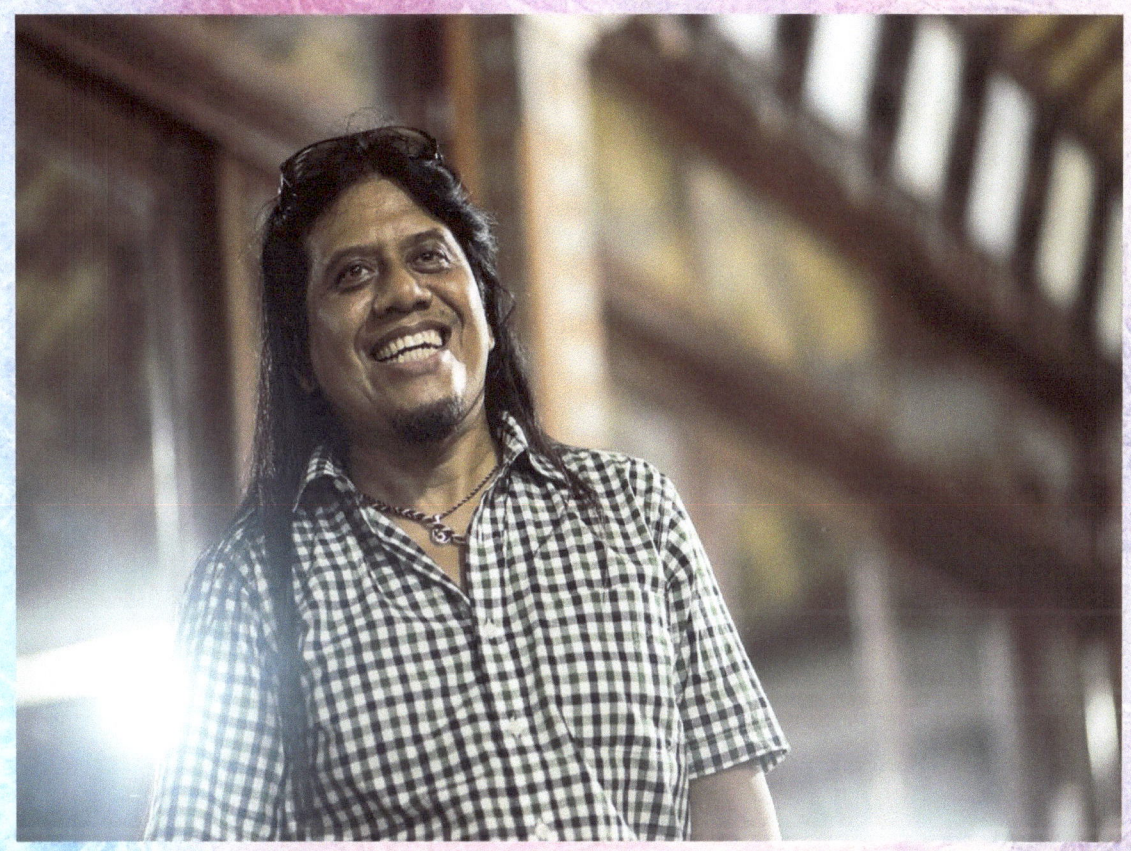

I Made Sidia is a Balinese Wayang Puppeteer. He is one of Bali's most acclaimed shadow artists. He has worked with hundreds of school students from around the globe, teaching the Wayang Kulit and the Kecak. teaching wayang puppetry, kayonan dances, Kecak dance and traditional makeup and costuming.

"Do not go where the path may lead, go instead where there is no path and leave a trail." Ralph Waldo Emerson

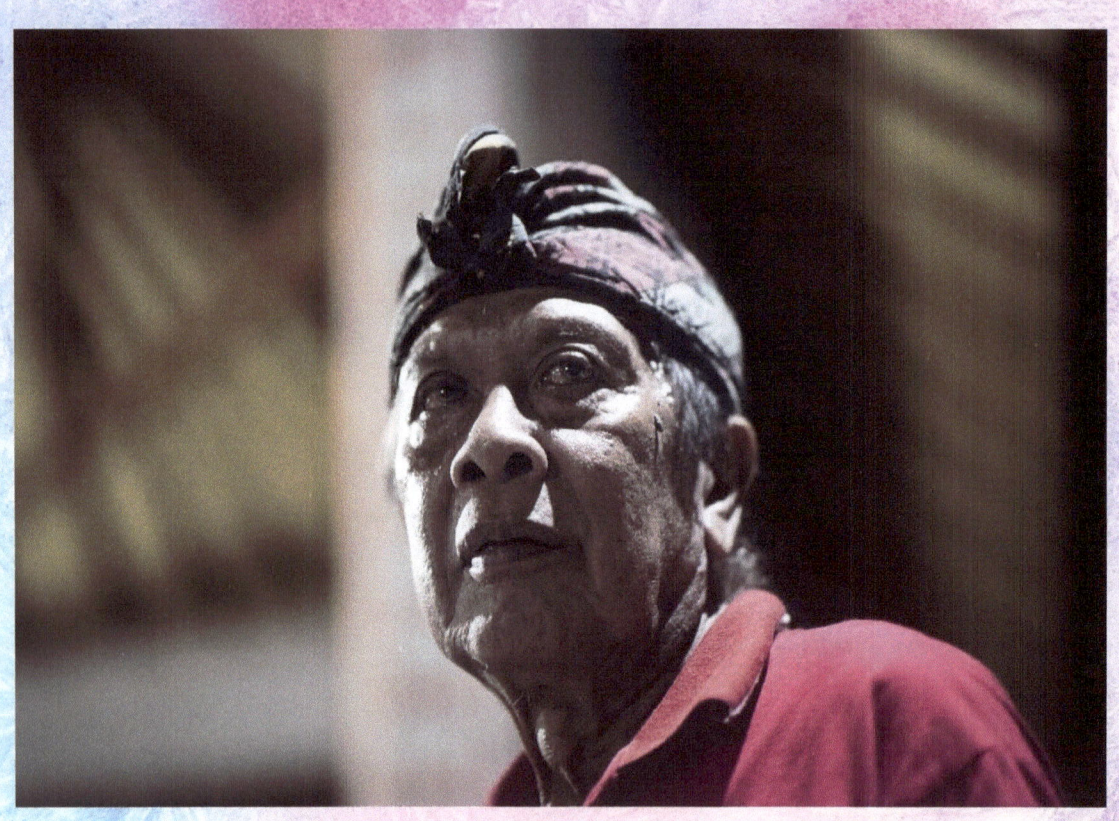

I Made Sijia .. mentor to his family who dance, play music and do puppetry for the community and internationally.

"Every story I create, creates me. I write to create myself." Octavia E. Butler

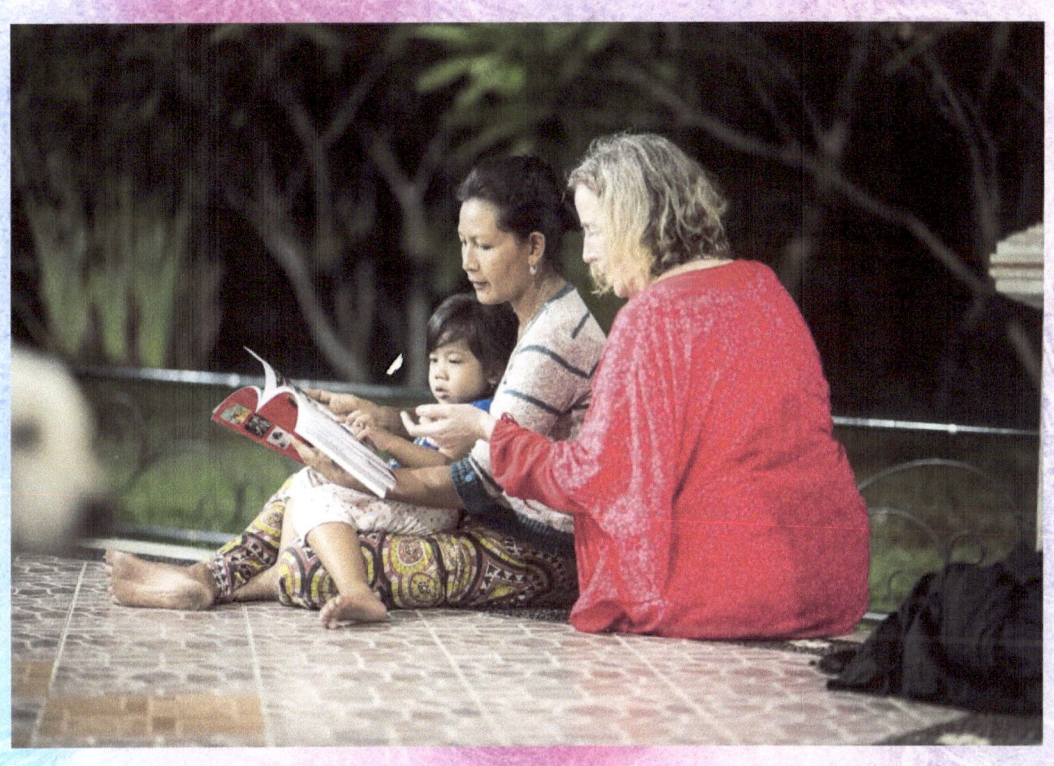

Della and Wayan Swastini sharing the book "Bali Feeds the Soul" created from the Spirit of Writing and Art in Bali 2015.

Bali dancers learn the craft as children and even in the womb they are played Balinese music. They are taught to dance with their hands before they can walk. Official training as a Bali dancer starts as young as 7. In Balinese dance the movement is closely associated with the rhythms produced by the gamelan, a musical ensemble specific to Java and Bali.

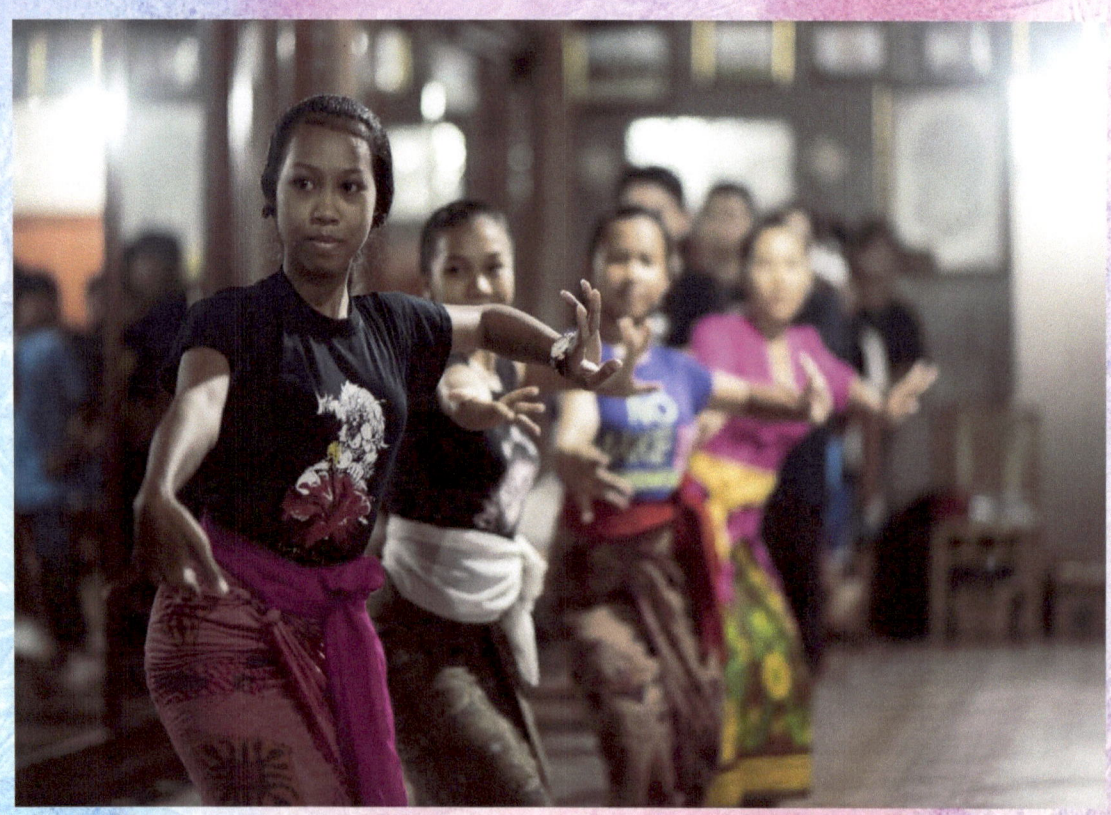

Students at the Sagga Paripurna in Bali.

"We should consider every day lost on which we have not danced at least once."
— Friedrich Nietzsche

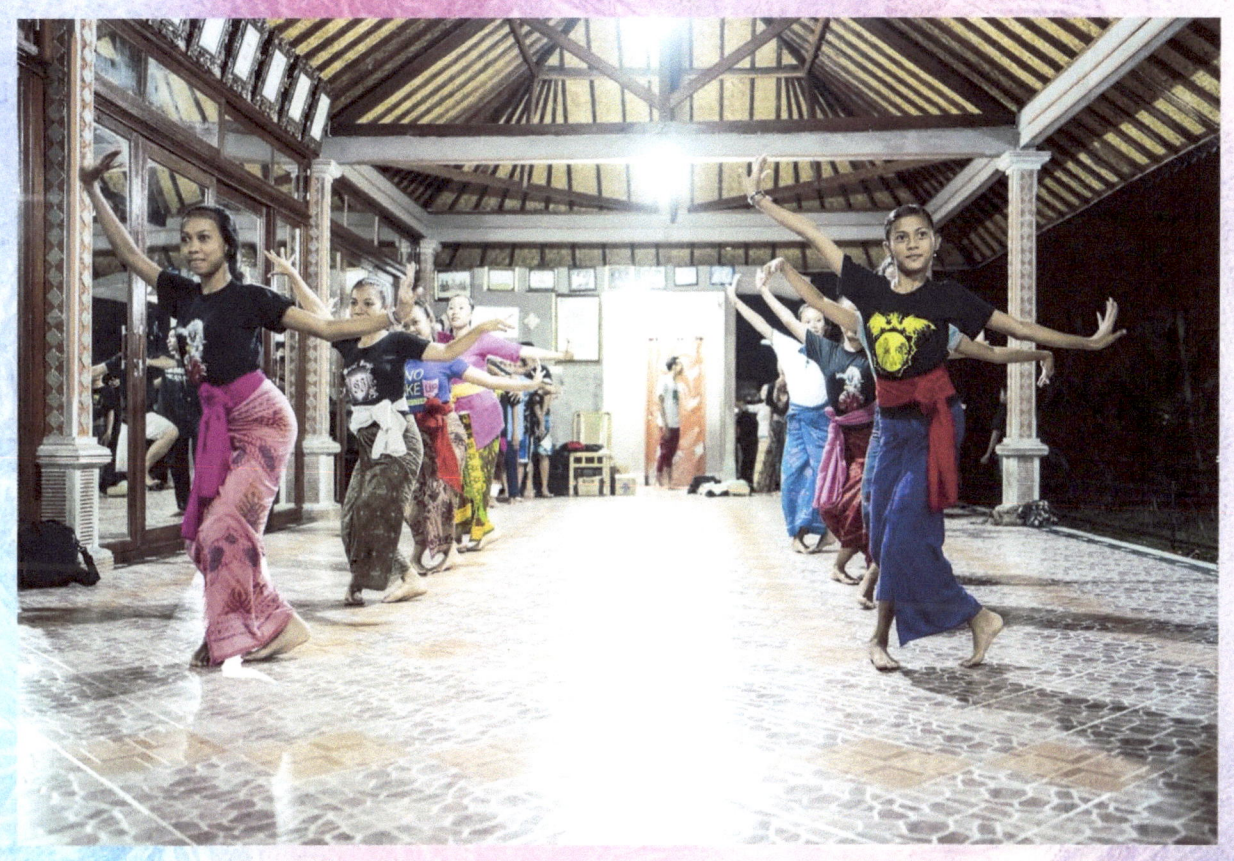

Students practising at the Sangha Paripurna dance company in Bali.

"The future belongs to those who believe in the beauty of their dreams." Eleanor Roosevelt

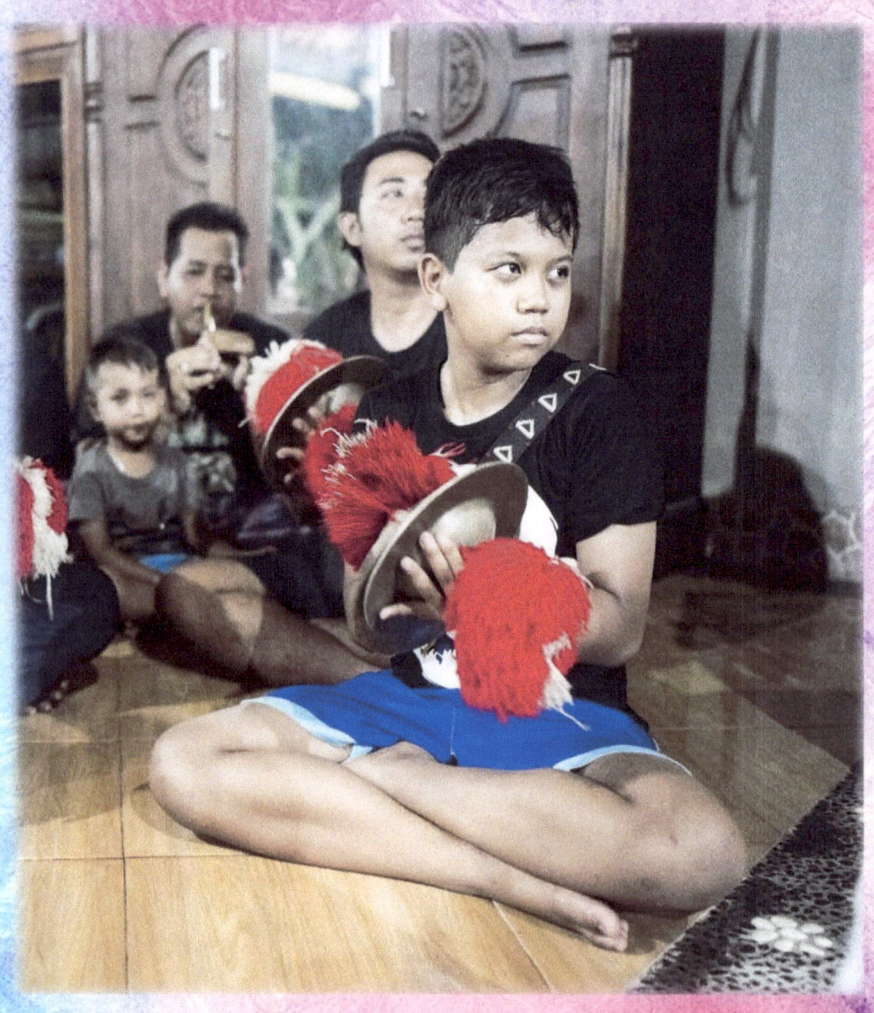

I Kadek Sugi Sidiarta

Barong is a lion-like creature and character in the mythology of Bali, Indonesia. He is the king of the spirits, leader of the hosts of good, and enemy of Rangda, the demon queen and mother of all spirit guarders in the mythological traditions of Bali.

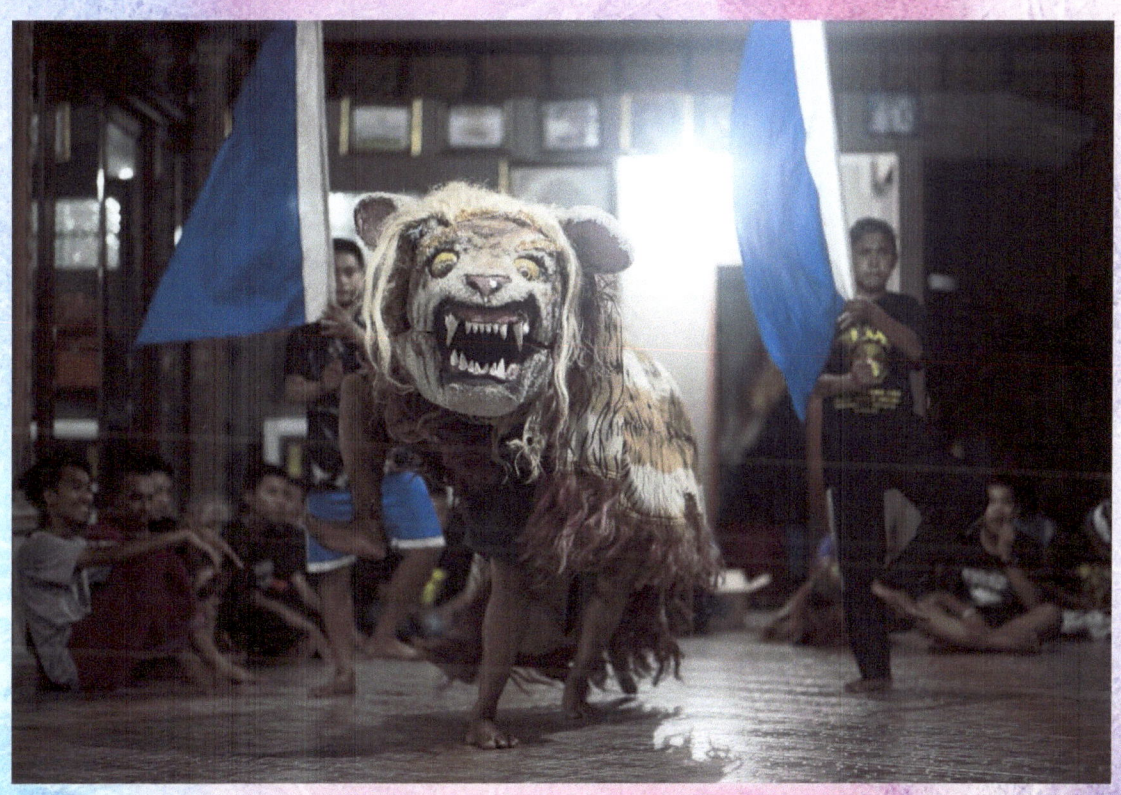

Dancing the Barong at Saaga Paripurna

The term Barong derives from the local term bahruang, which today corresponds to Indonesian word beruang which means "bear" - It refers to a good spirit, that took the form of an animal as the guardian of forest.

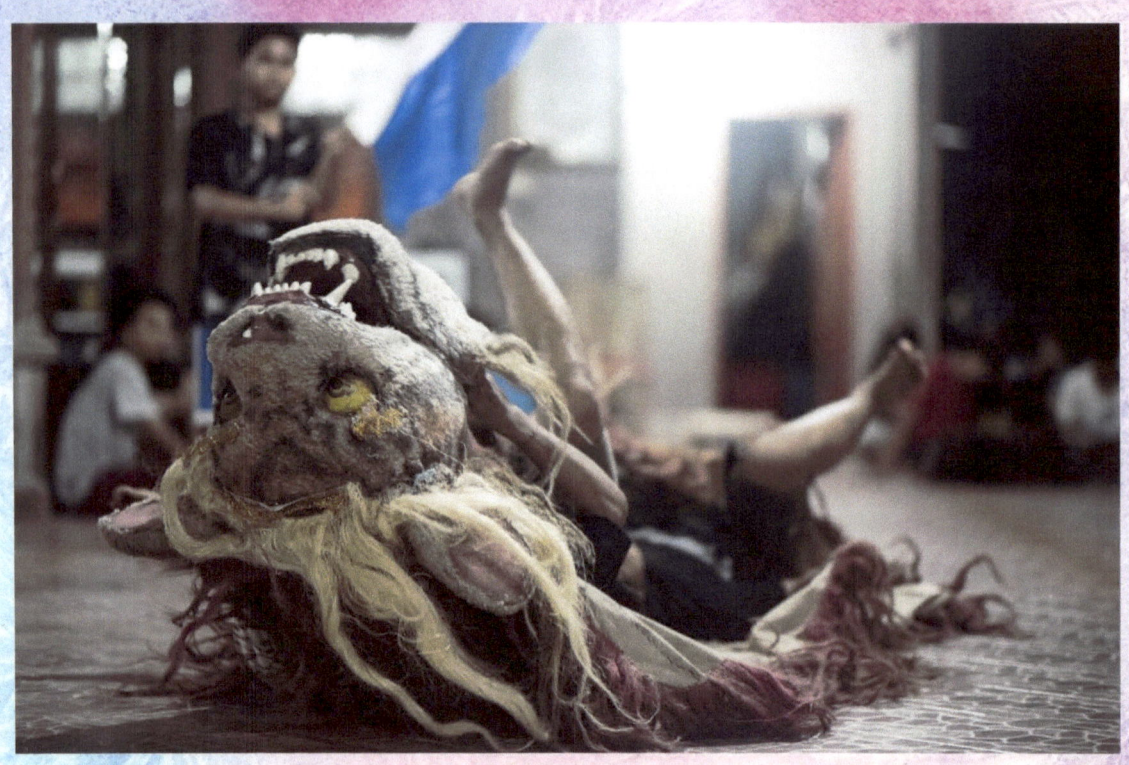

Rehearsal of the Barong dance at Sagga Paripurna. This is a playful moment.

"Where words leave us music begins"
Heinrich Heine

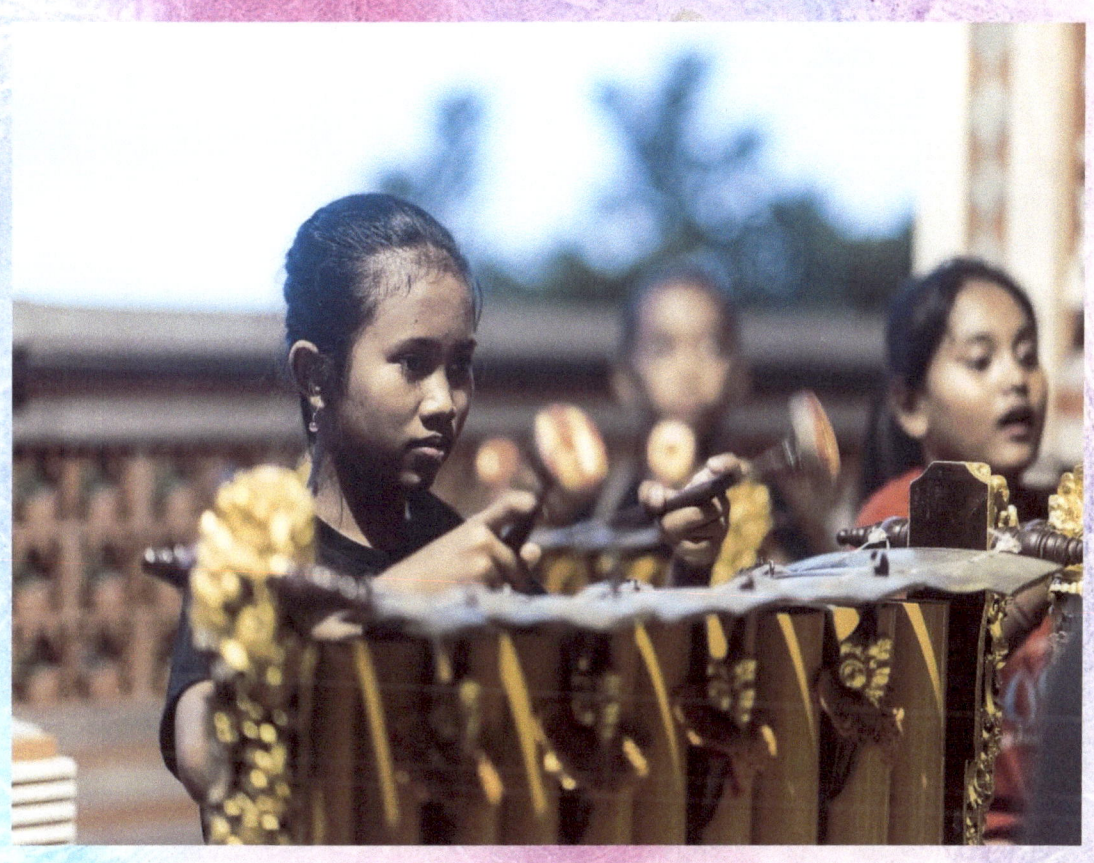

Student playing gamelan in Bali.

"Ah, music," he said, wiping his eyes. "A magic beyond all we do here!"
— J.K. Rowling

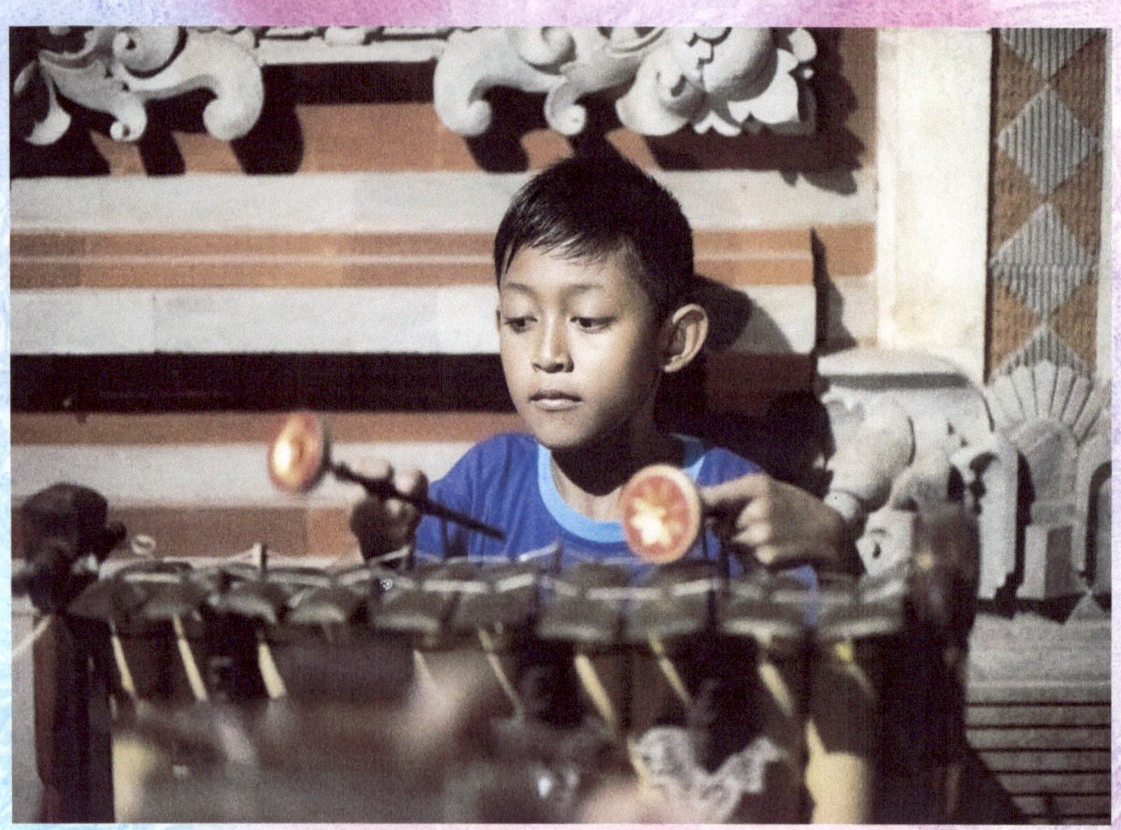

Student at the Sagga Paripurna in Bali.

"Dancing is like dreaming with your feet!" - Constanze

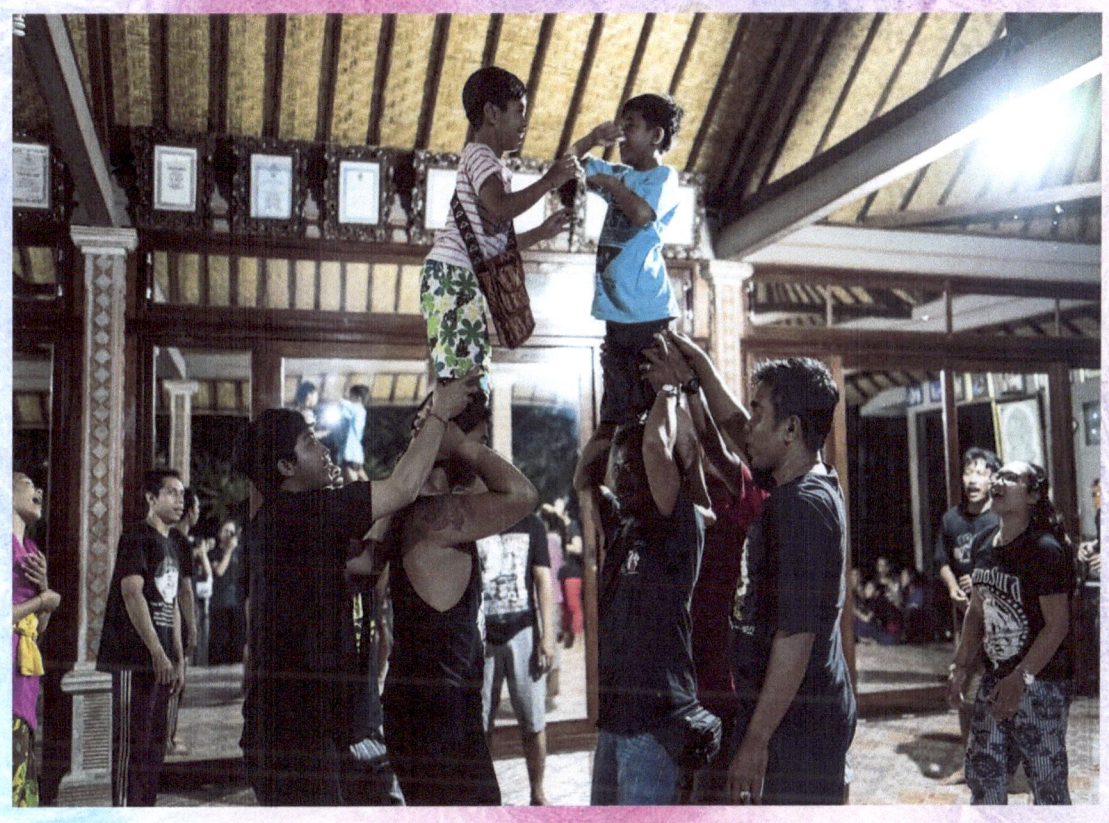

Students from the Sagga Paripurna rehearsing for a production.

Wayan Swastini and I Made Sijia dancing at the opening of the Spirit of Writing and Art in Ubud, Bali.

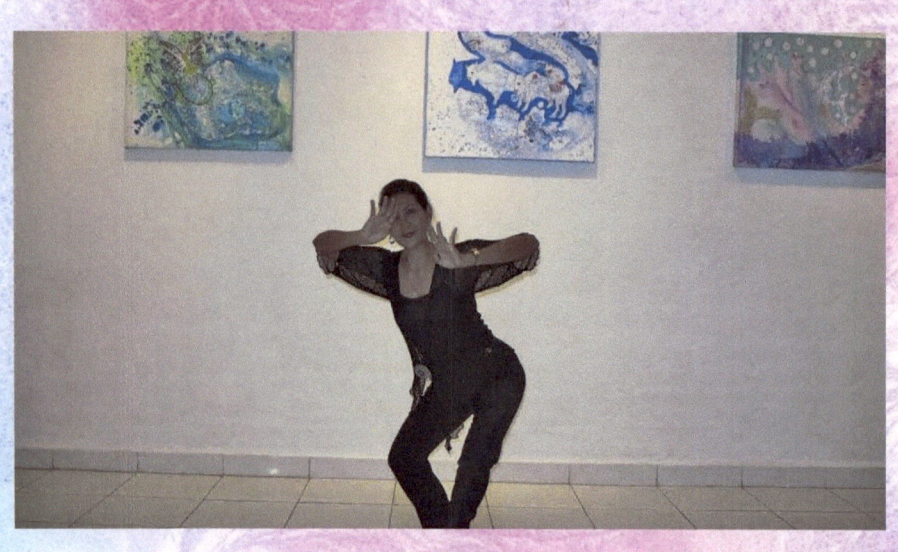

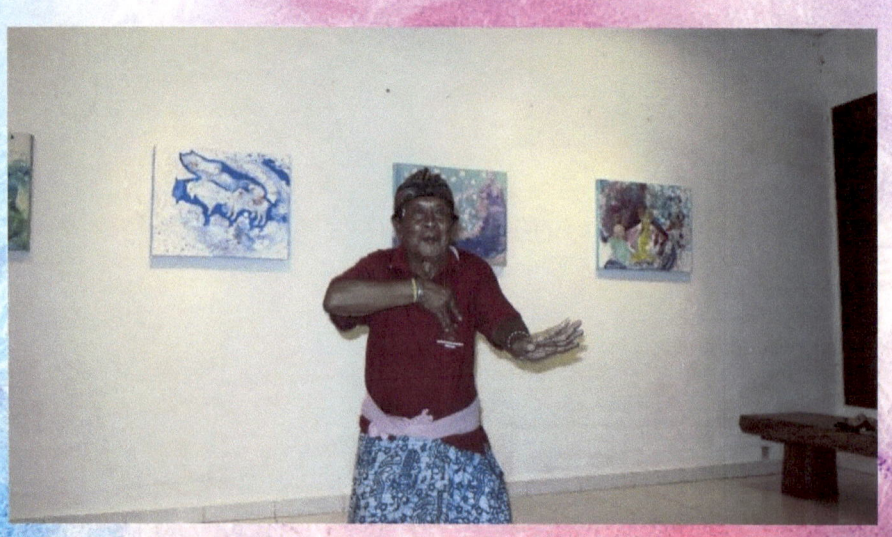

"A dream doesn't become reality through magic; it takes sweat, determination and hard work." Colin Powell

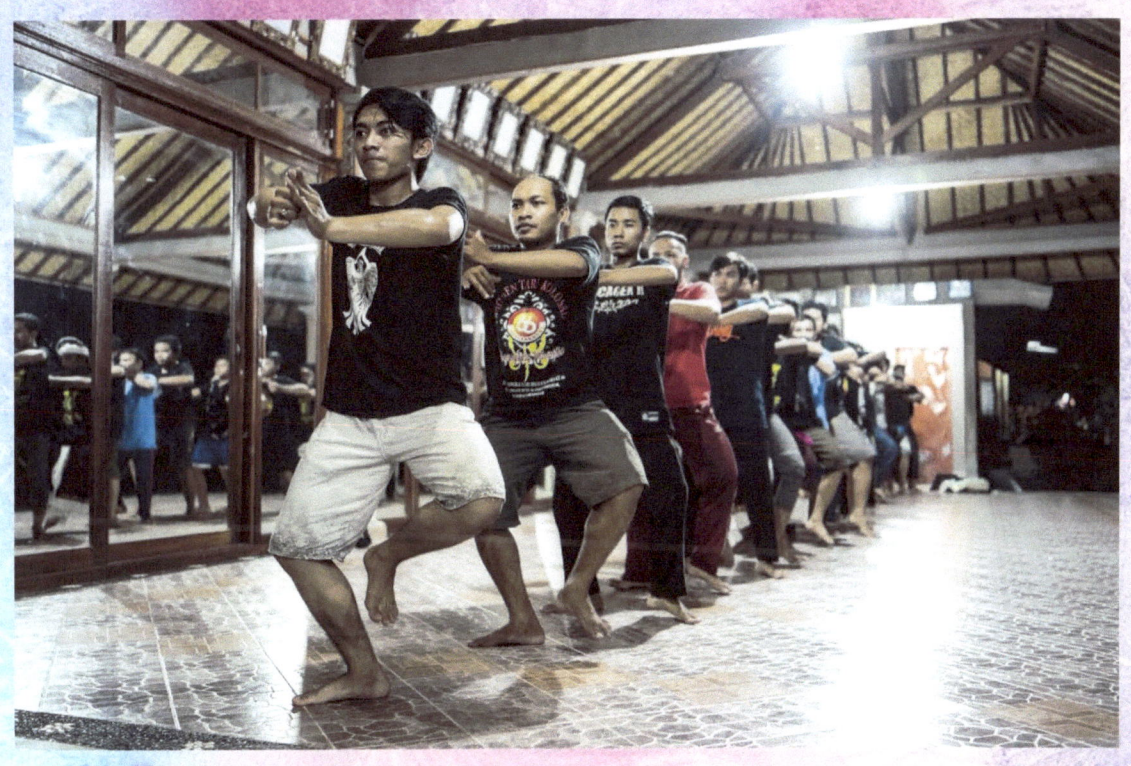

Students peforming for upcoming show.

At the Spirit of Writing and Art prayers were offered , and dancing flowed

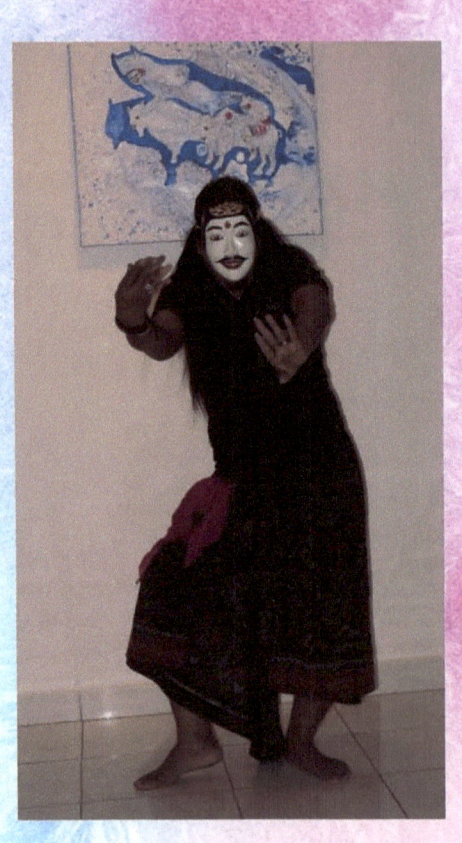
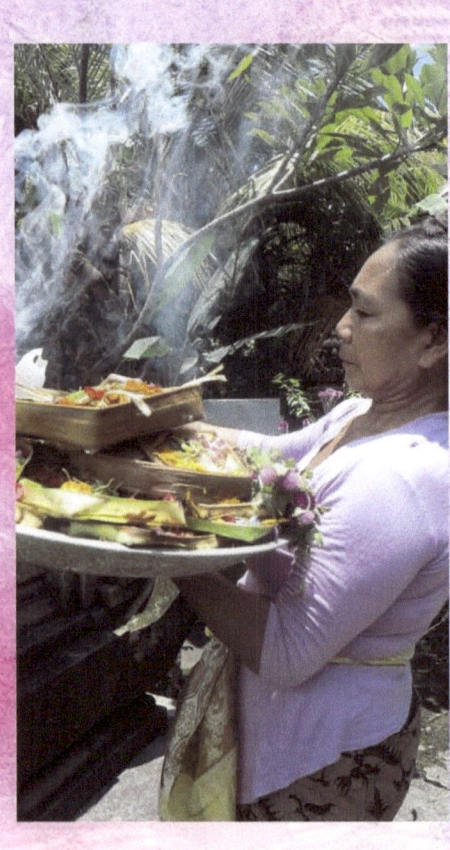

"Life is the dancer and you are the dance."
— Eckhart Tolle

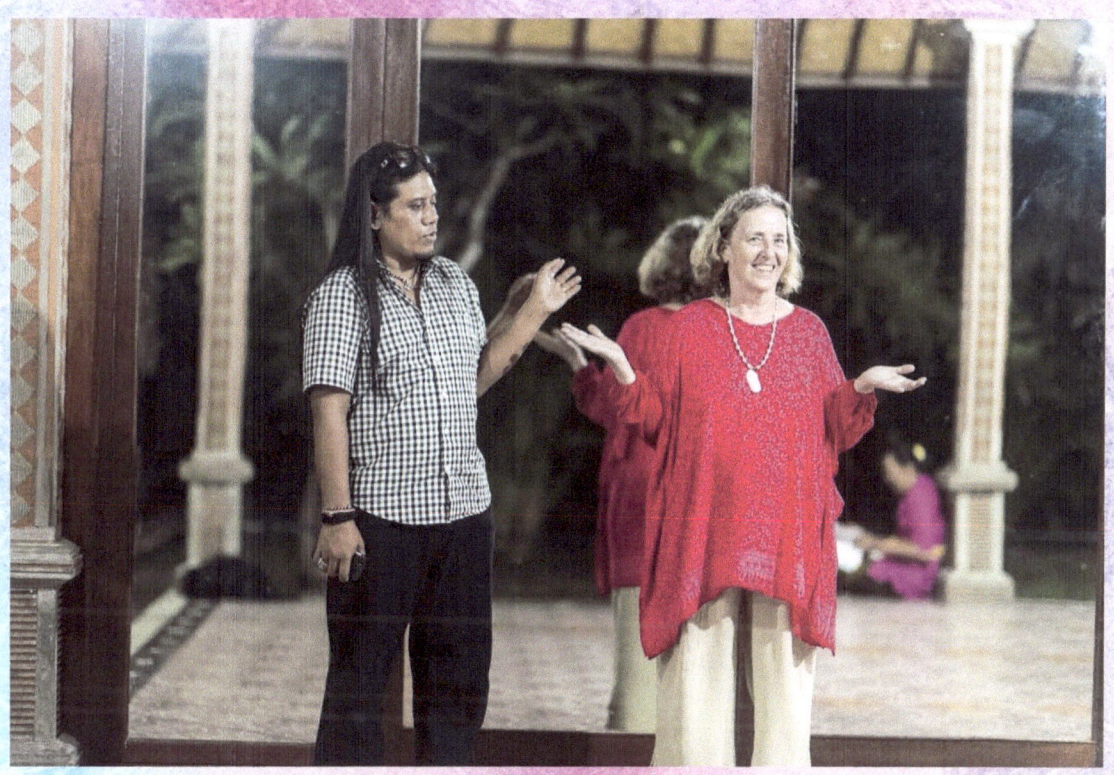

I Made Sidia and Della Burford. There families met in Sweden in the 1980's at the Globetree Conference at the concert hall in Stockholm. Della and Dale have visited Bali now 5 times and each time look forward to seeing Made Sidia and his beautiful famly.

Sharing the Dream

Della Burford created a Dream Wheel every year for 40 years and on them recorded her most important dreams. Many dreams were manifested into books, performances and paintings and shared internationally. Dale Bertrand helped in many aspects of the dream work. The painting of "Dream Wheels" amd Dream Keys" were both shown in Bali at Karja's Studio in a collaborative show swith Wayan Karja. Many friends attending including those in Making the Dream.

"The biggest adventure you can take is to live the life of your dreams."
Oprah Winfrey

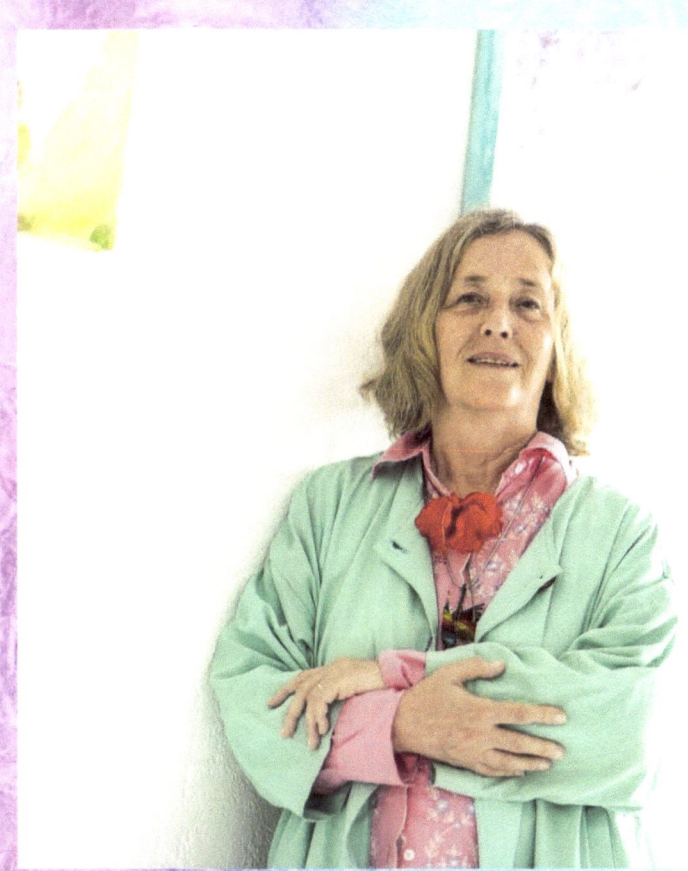

Della Burford in Bali at "Dream Wheels" show of paintings.

To keep dreams alive remember: "You and synchronicity are one" from the book "Dream Keys".

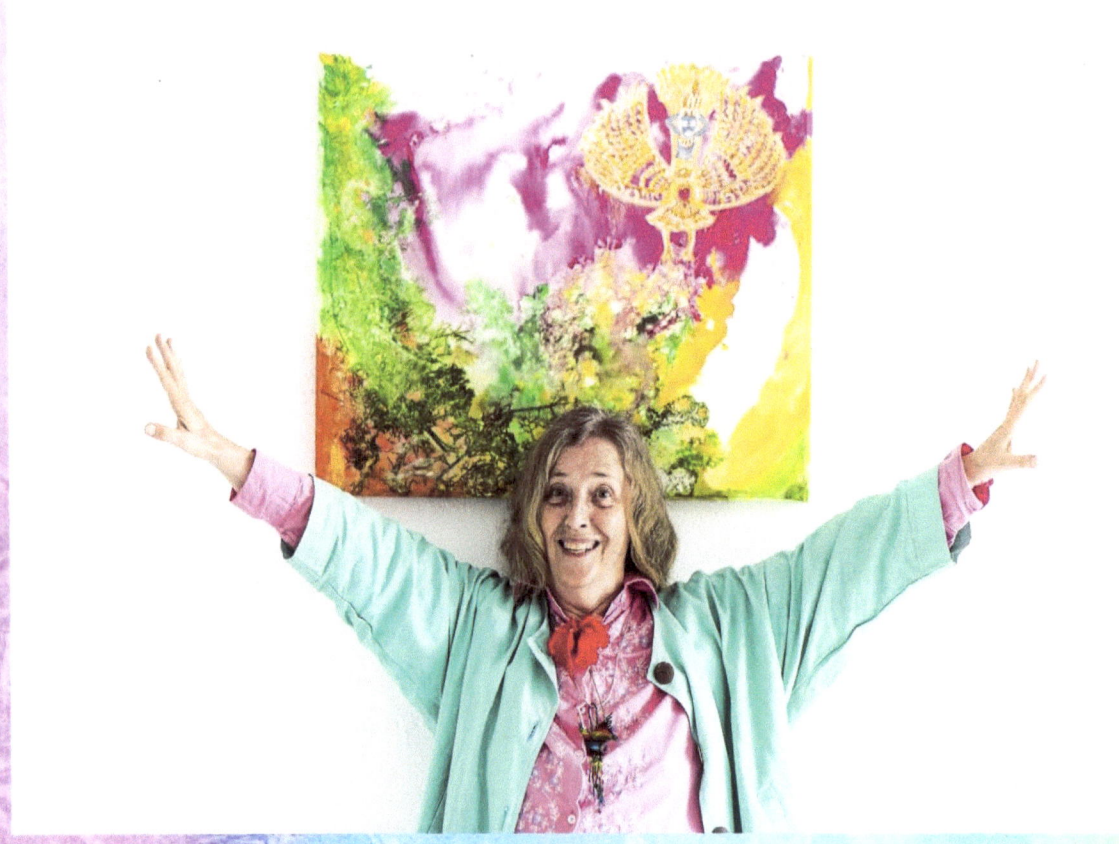

Della Burford in front of "Synchronicity".

To keep dreams alive remember:
"I and Nature are one, I love nature and am thankful for nature" from Dream Keys

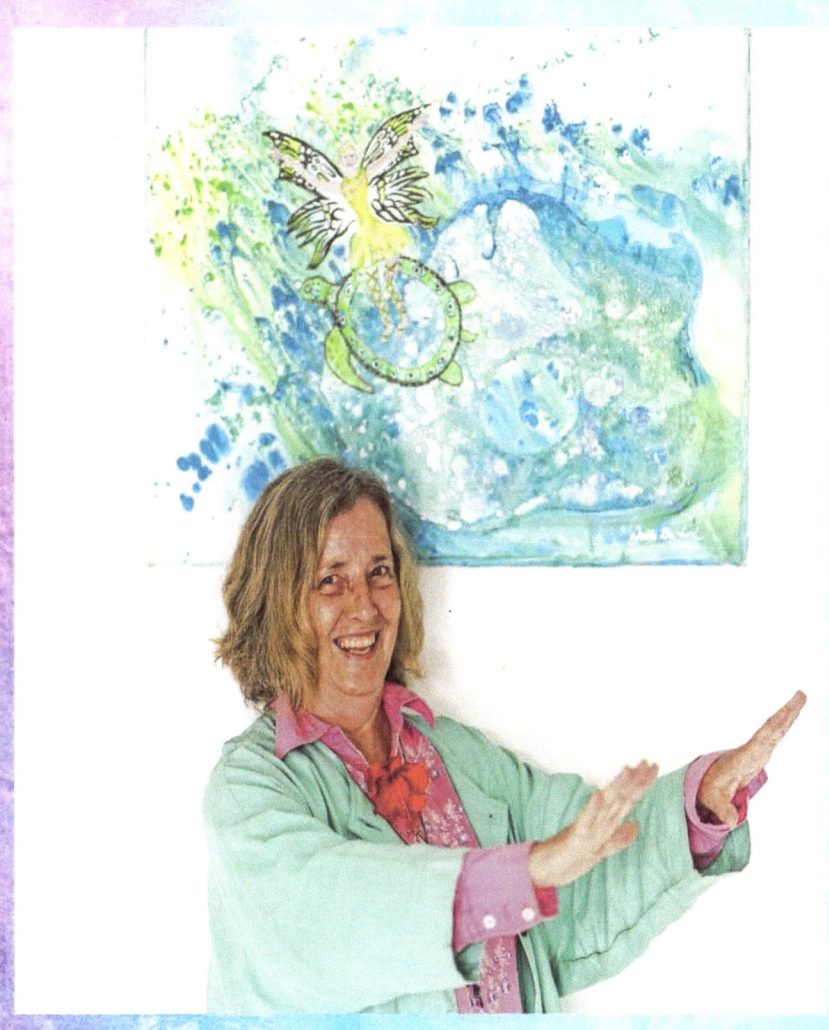

Della Burford with the Gaia Turtle painting.

To remember your dreams say: "I and story are one. I love story and give thanks for story" from the book "Dream Keys".

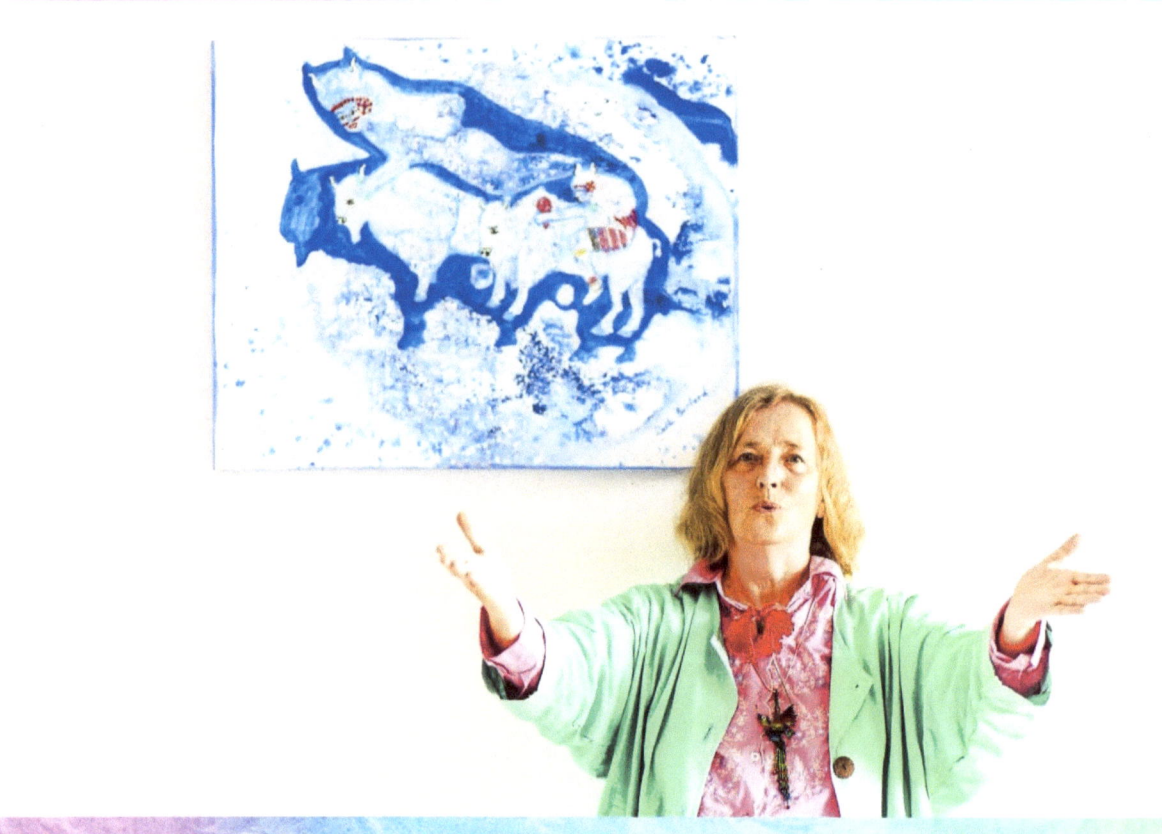

Della Burford with the "White Buffalo" painting.

To keep your dreams alive remember "
"I an intuition are one. I love intuition and give thanks for intuition" from "Dream Keys" by Della Burford.

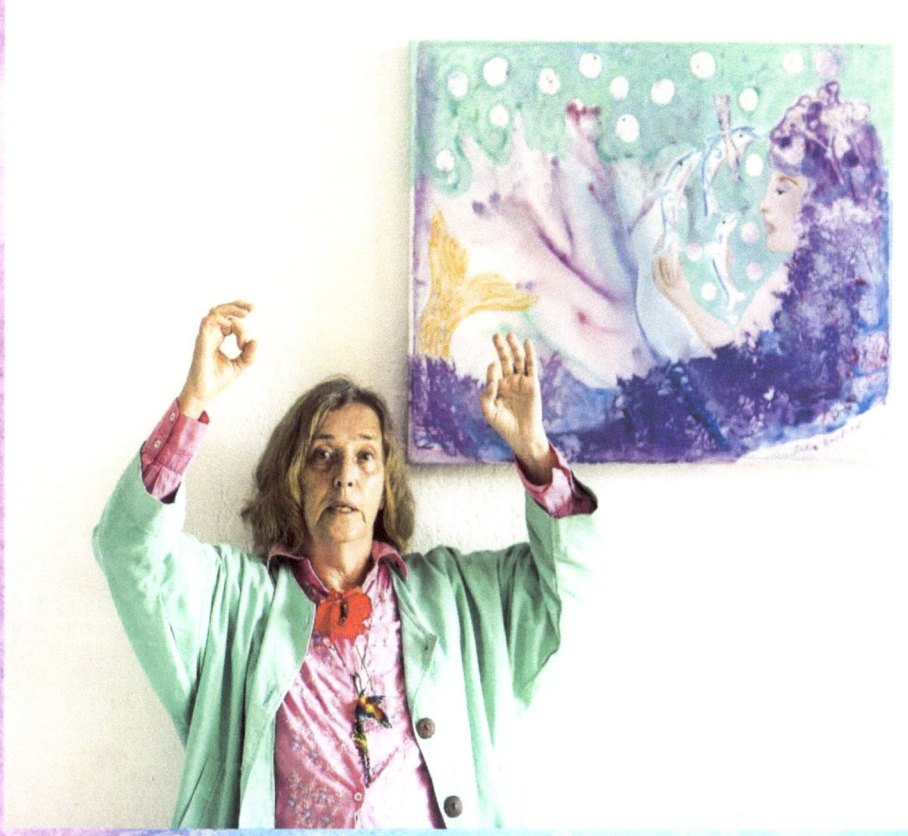

Della Burford with the "White Dolphin" painting.

To keep your dreams alive remember"
"I and wisdom are one. I love wisdom and give thanks for wisdom" from "Dream Keys" by Della Burford

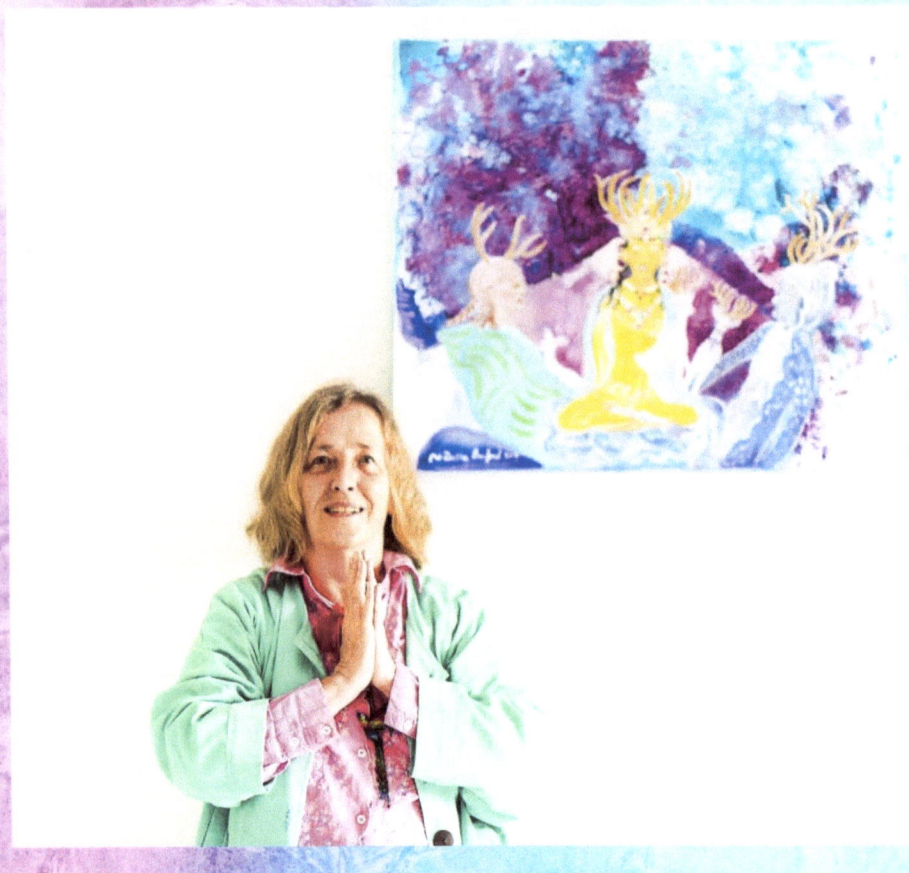

Della Burford with the "White Deer Goddesses"

At the "Dream Keys" opening with Leema, Freeman and friends.

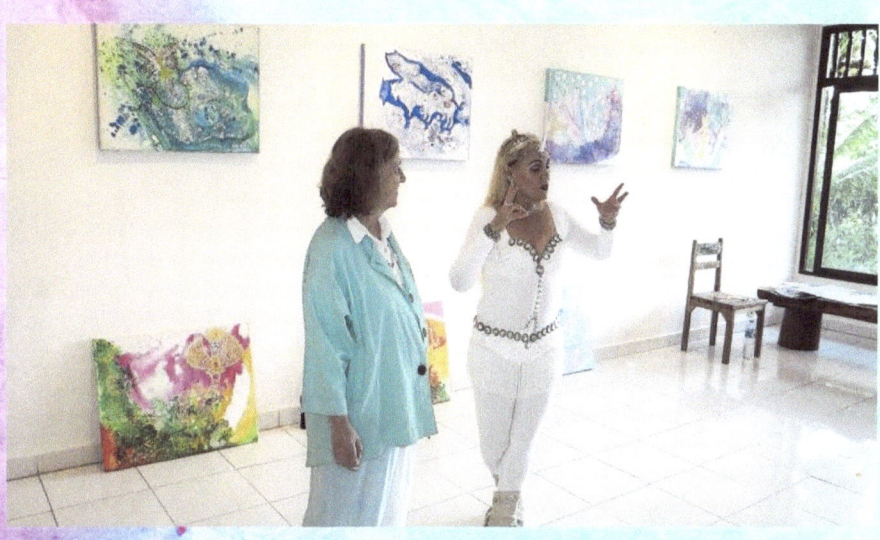

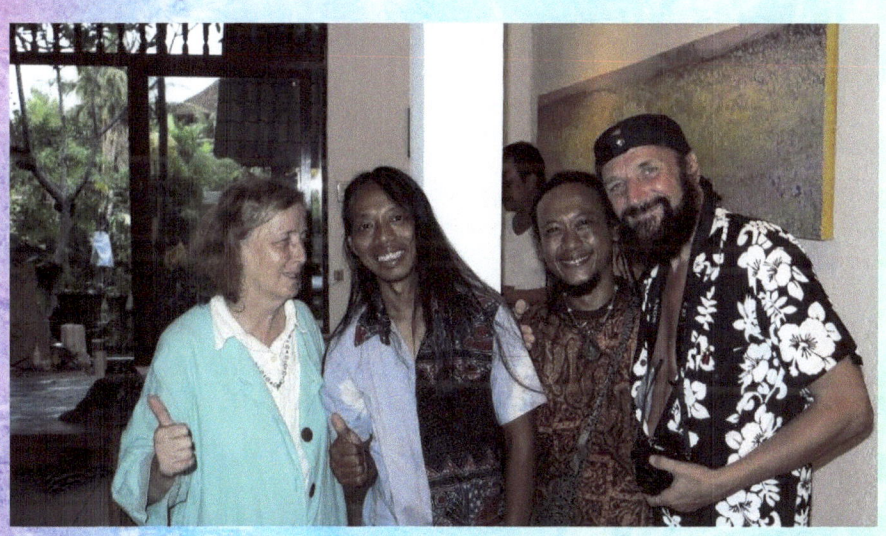

Della at the Dream Keys opening speaking about how her paintings came from dreams. Also in photo below Ken, Della, Leema (who danced the unicorn) and Ayden who was choosing music for our workshops and playing instuments.

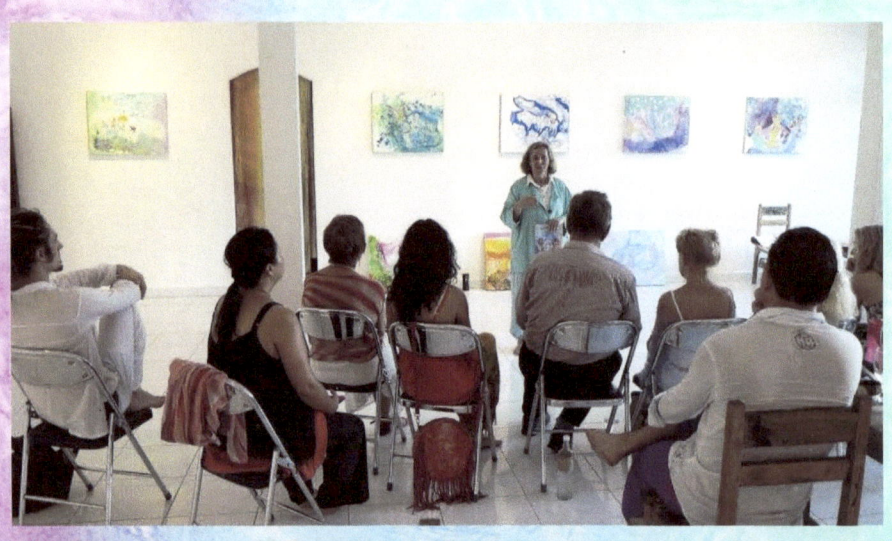

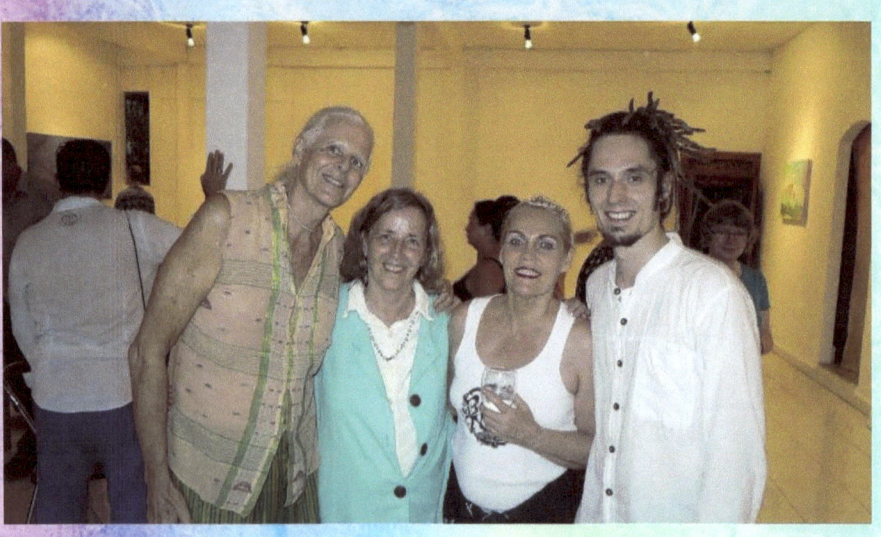

"The greatest healing therapy is friendship and love." Hubert H. Humphrey

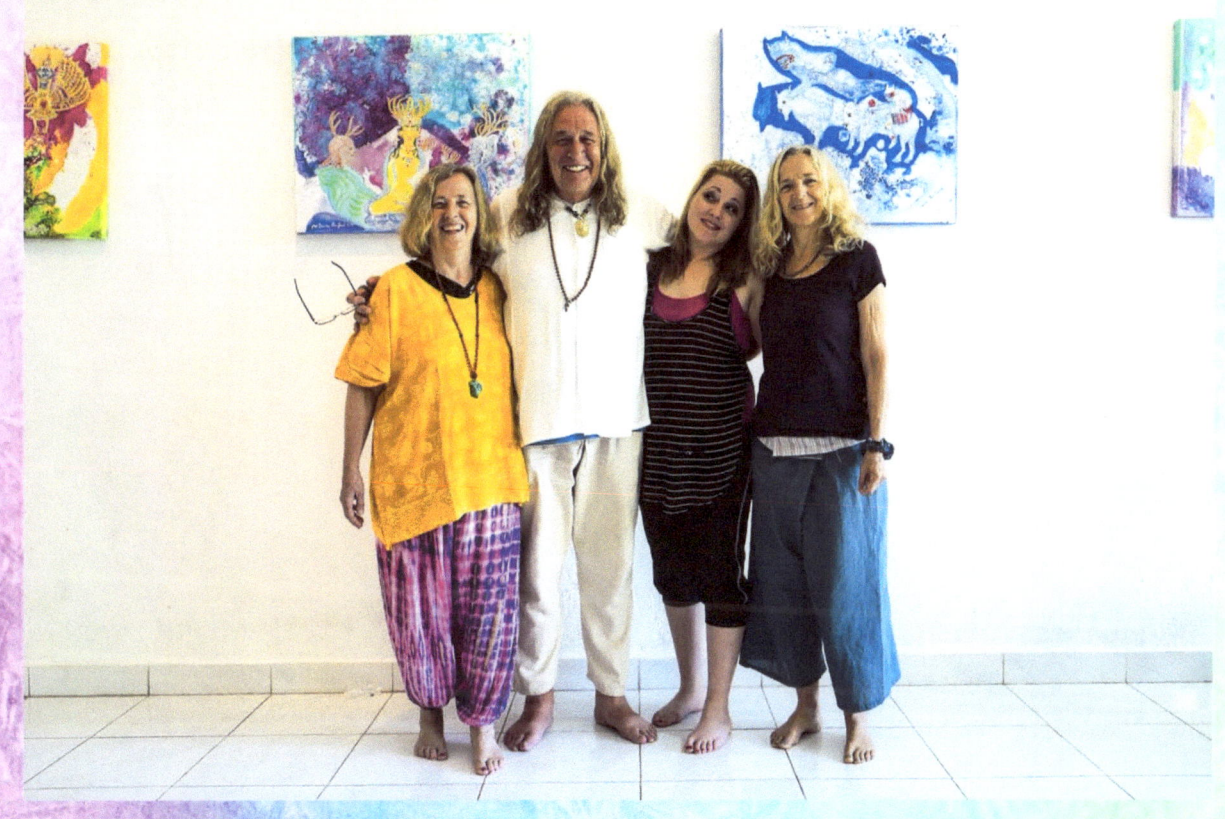

Family in Bali.. Della Burford, Dale Bertrand, Holly Yurxa and Norah Burford.

"I have collected meaningful dreams and recorded them in my diary, and have created "Dream Wheels" as a form of celebration and way of honoring my dreams for thirty six years. The symbols become a portal back to the dream." Della Burford

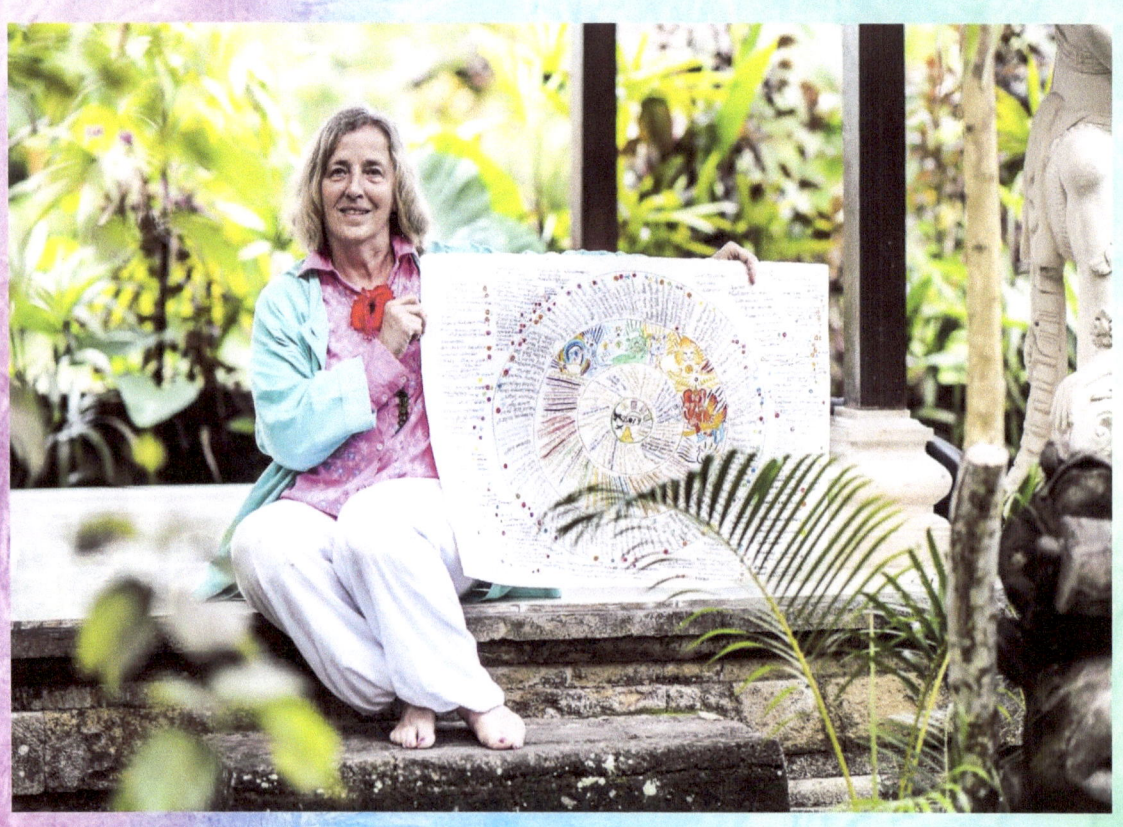

Della Burford with one of her Dream Wheels.

"Life is full of beauty. Notice it. Notice the bumble bee, the small child, and the smiling faces. Smell the rain, and feel the wind. Live your life to the fullest potential, and fight for your dreams." Ashley Smith

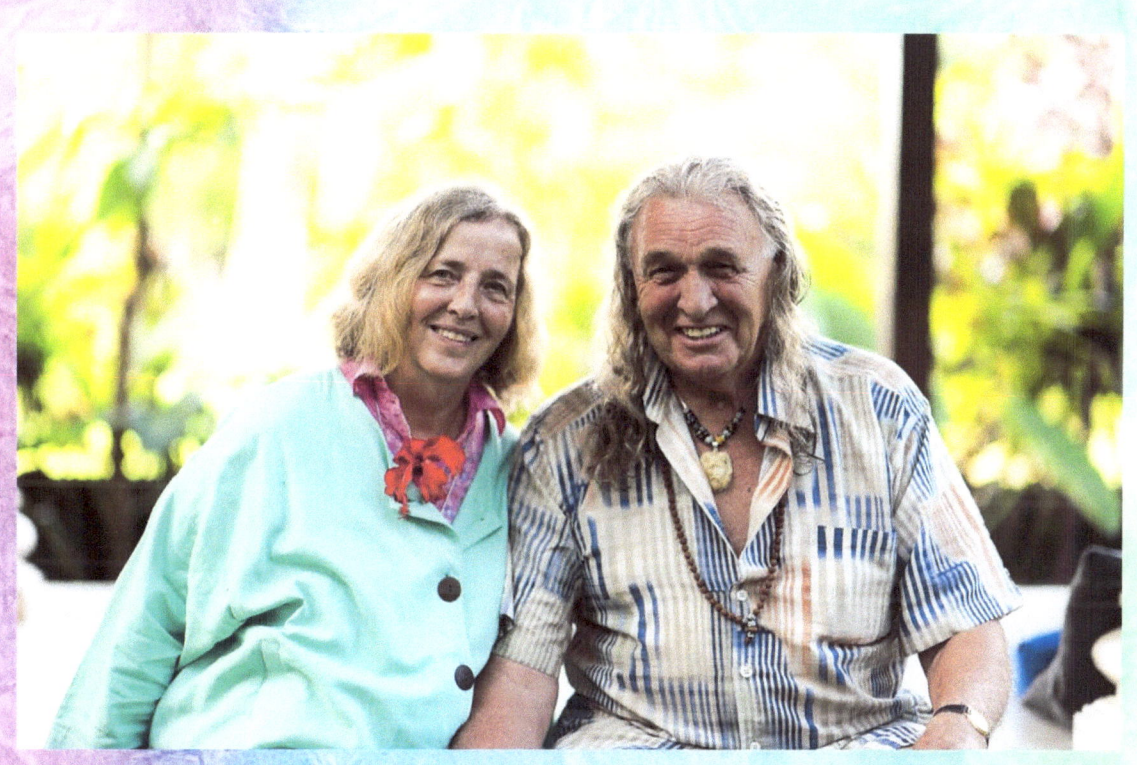

Della Burford and Dale Bertrand – hosts of the Spirit of Writing and Art.

Making Dreams

Many friends came to be part of the Spirit of Writing and Art and made their dreams. Thanks to Fabrizio Belardetti for photogrpahy, thanks to Norah for coordinating, Wayan Karja for his villa and studio and mentoring. Thanks Dale for sharing Medicine Wheels and photos. Sylke Gande – Sacred Art, Ayden Graham for music, Leema Graham for dance, & Charlyne Chiasson for Feng Shui. Thanks to Grace Po for painting, Wallace Murray for painting and also Saharnaz Fara for a yoga class, Eric Bobrow, Holly Yurxa and Warren Burford for joining us. Thanks Dewa, Wayan & Newman. Thanks to Michelle Pettit at Pelanghi School and Ketut Gina Indiyaran and Christina Hatala at Villa Flamboyant in Ahmed. Thanks to everyone at Santra Putra including Puta and the wonderful cooks for our Dream breakfasts in Ubud. Everyone has explored their own dreams and helped fulfill the big dream of holding this retreat in Bali.

Stretching Della's painting for the Dream Keys exhibition with Wayan Karja at the Spirit of Writing and Art.

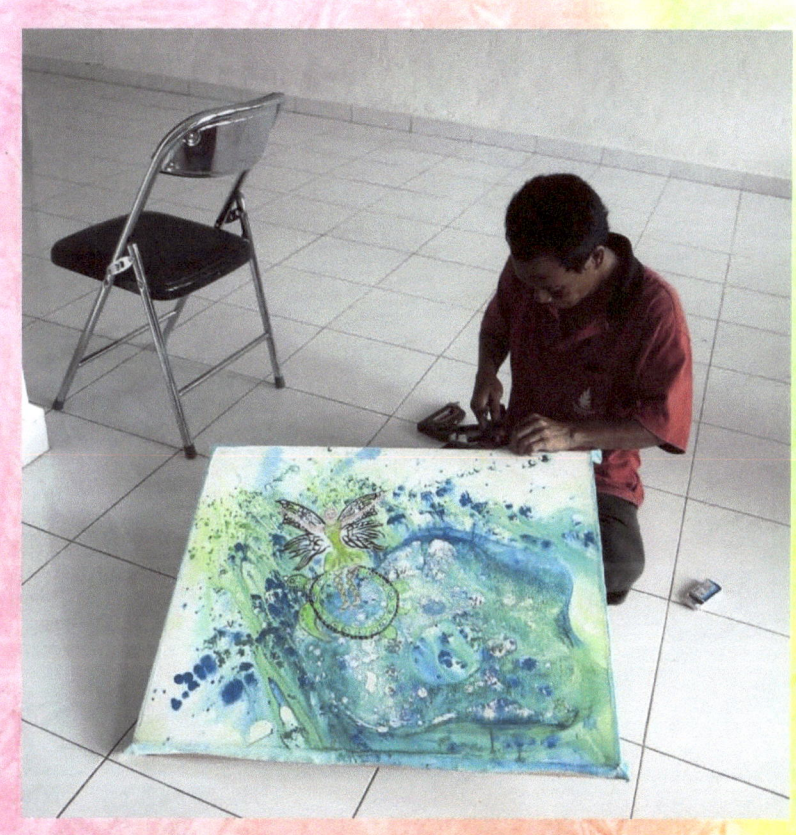

At Santra Putra villa.

Pura Besakih is a complex made up of twenty-three temples that sit on parallel ridges. It has stepped terraces and flights of stairs which ascend to a number of courtyards and brick gateways that in turn lead up to the main spire or Meru structure, which is called Pura Penataran Agung.

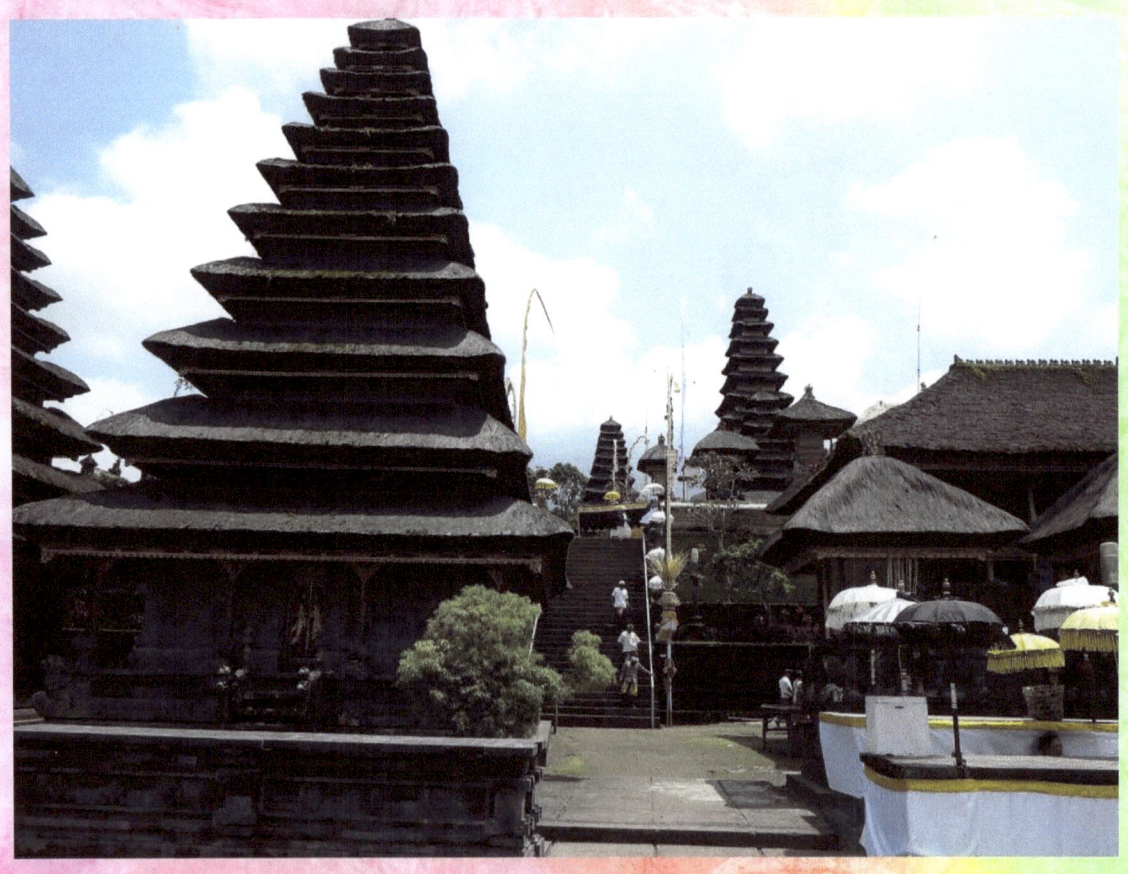

Our group from Spirit of Writing and Art had a field trip to the Sacred Pura Besakih.

Festival time .. a Fire Dance that happens every 100 years.

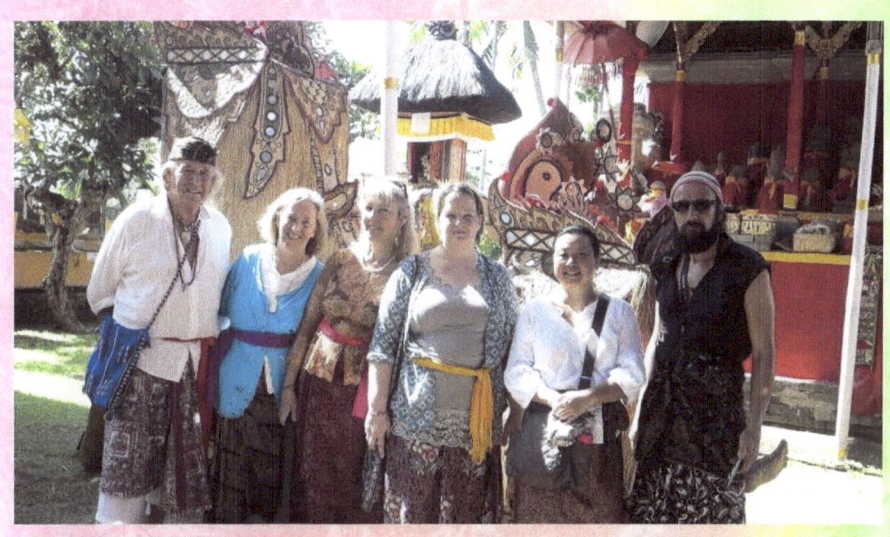

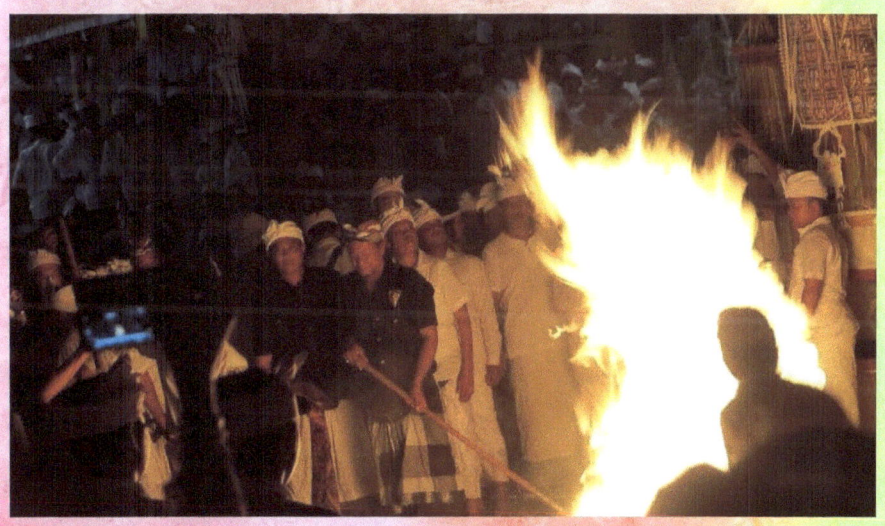

"I think when you move past your fear and you go after your dreams wholeheartedly, you become free."
LL Cool J

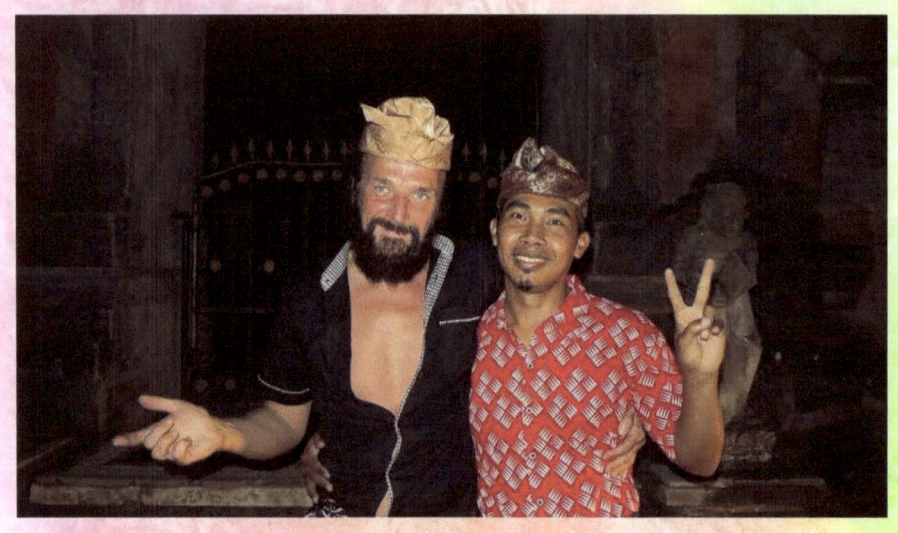

Free man and New man Nyoman) !

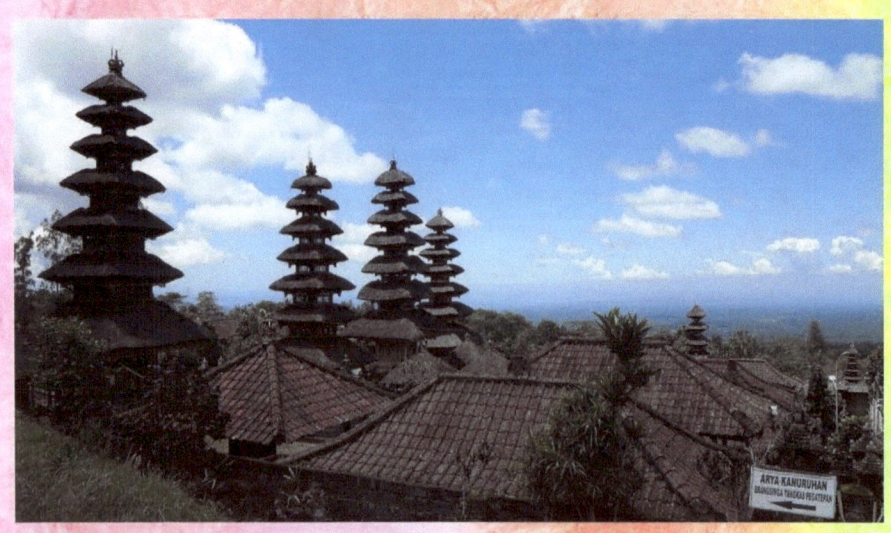

"I think fitness is important. I think a healthy lifestyle is important. I think putting positive energy out there is important and just staying connected with the people." LL Cool J

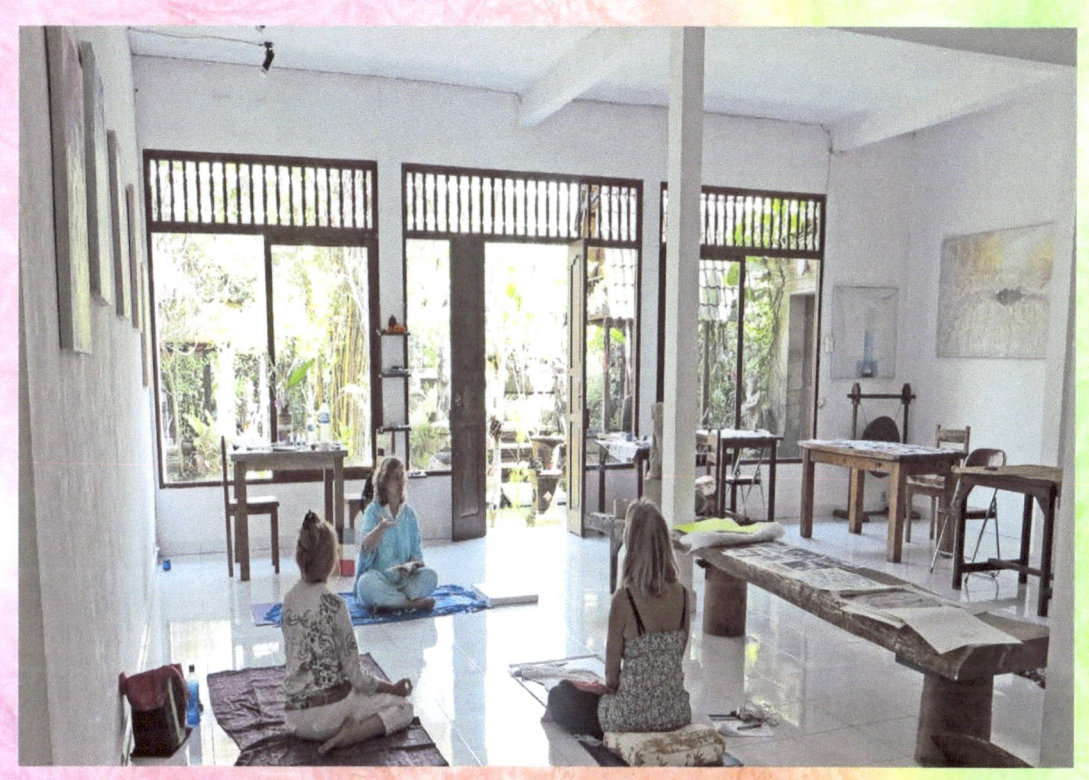

Acu- yoga class with Della at Karja's studio in Bali.

Charlyne Chiasson sharing her proof of her new Feng Shui book for professionals that will be published in 2017.

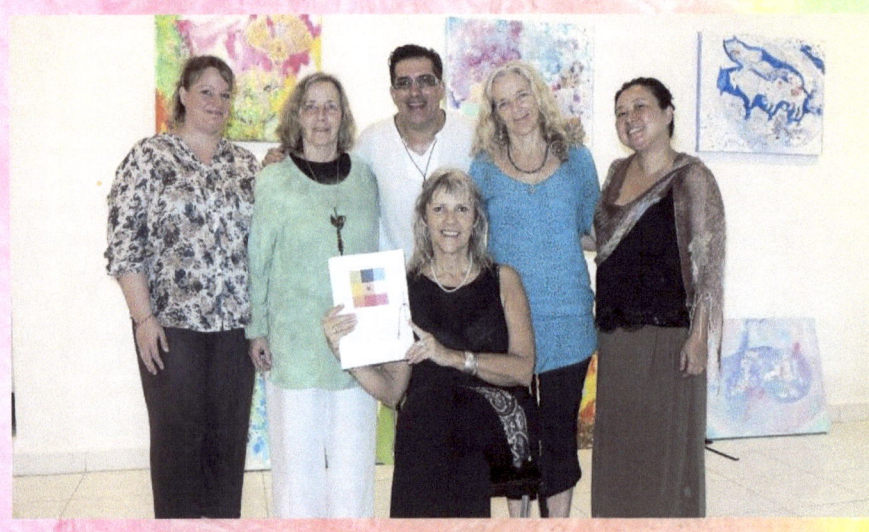

Charlyne was sharing her knowledge of Chinese Astrlogy and Feng Shui at the Spirit of Writing and Art in 2016.

"What i like about photographs is that they capture a moment that's gone forever, impossible to reproduce."
— Karl Lagerfeld

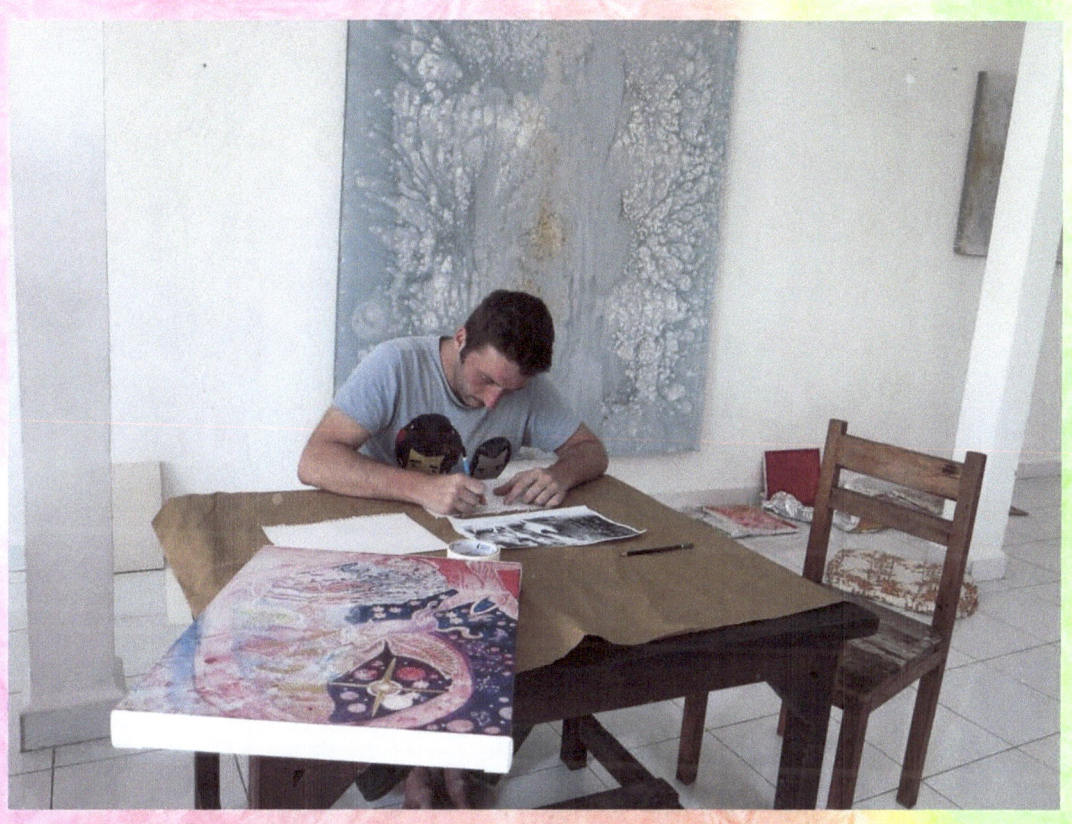

Able to photograph and capture a moment of our photographer Fabrizio Belardetti doing some art at the Spirit of Writing and Art in Bali 2015.

"Life isn't about finding yourself.
Life is about creating yourself."
George Bernard Shaw

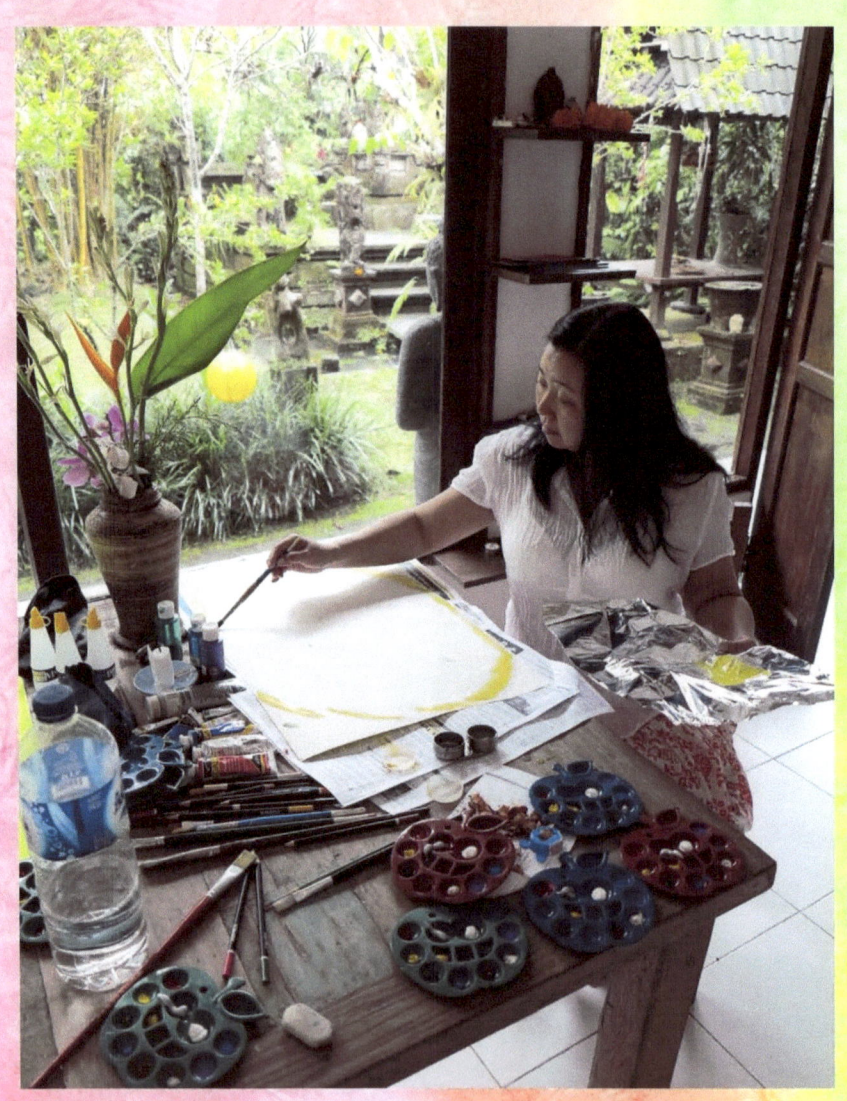

Grace Po painting at the Spirit of Writing and Art 2015.

Wayan Karja, who is an international artist, was mentoring some of the students at the Spirit of Writing and Art. They really enjoyed his wise advice.

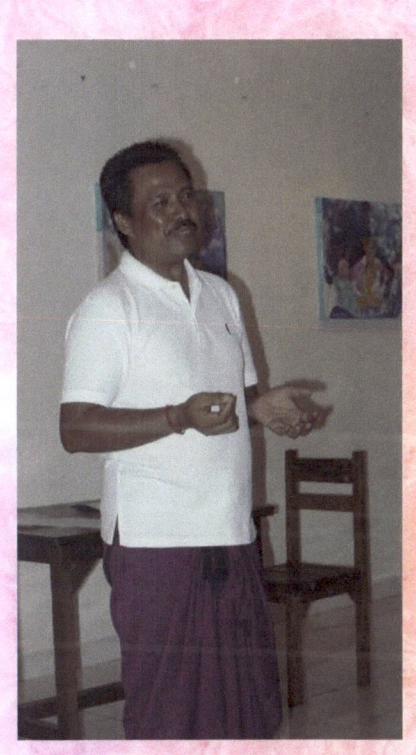
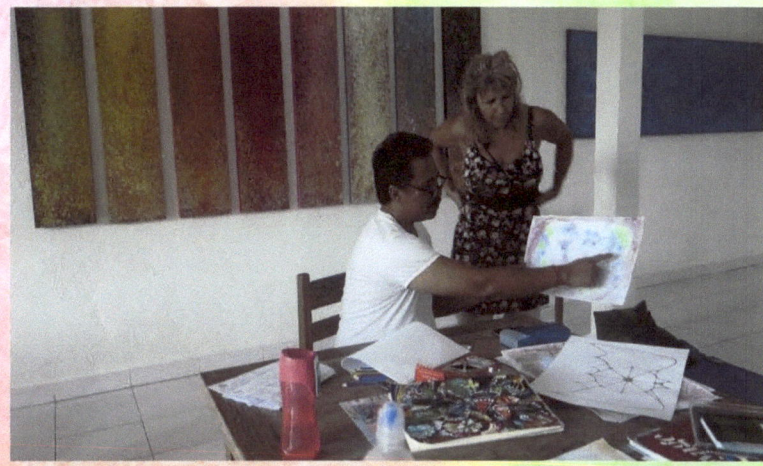
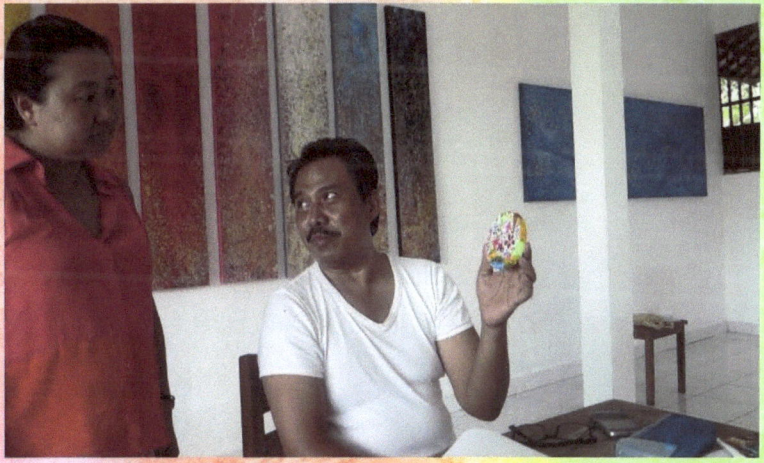

"The real ornament of woman is her character, her purity." Mahatma Ghandi

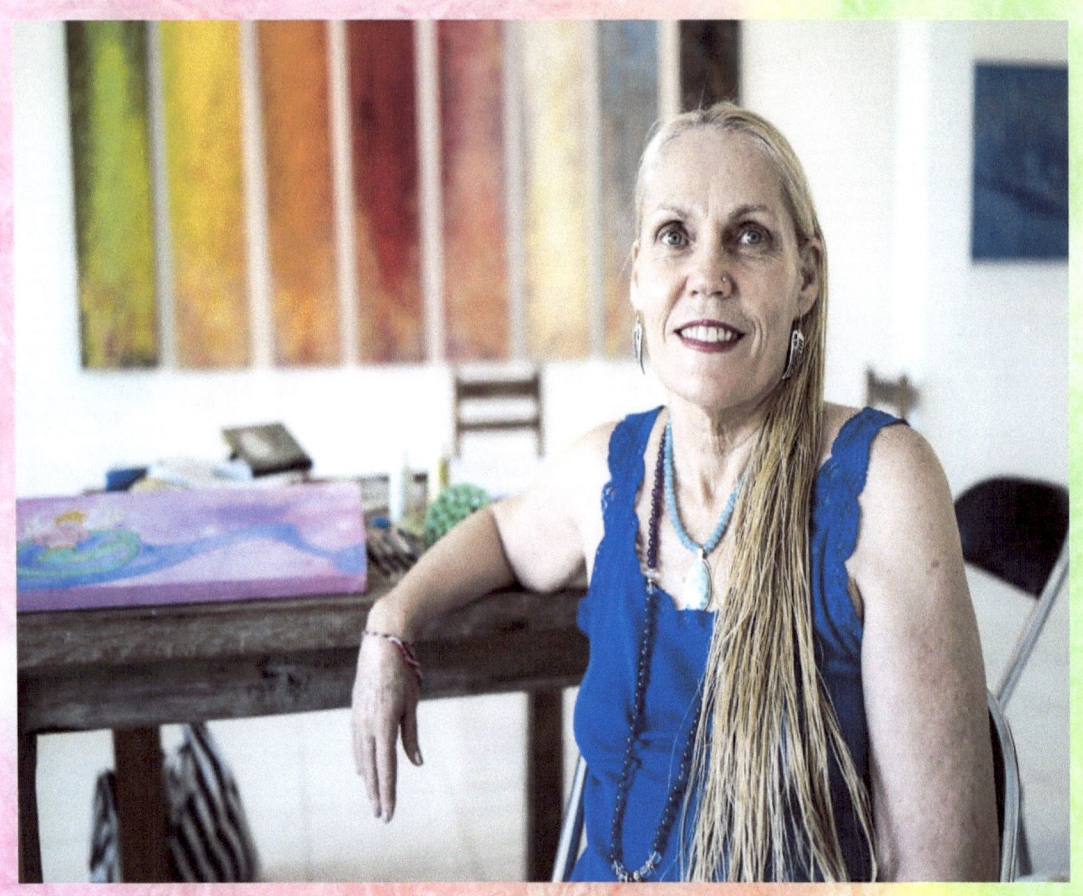

Leema Graham at the Spirit of Writing and Art in Bali.

"If we have no peace, it is because we have forgotten we belong to each other."
Mother Theresa

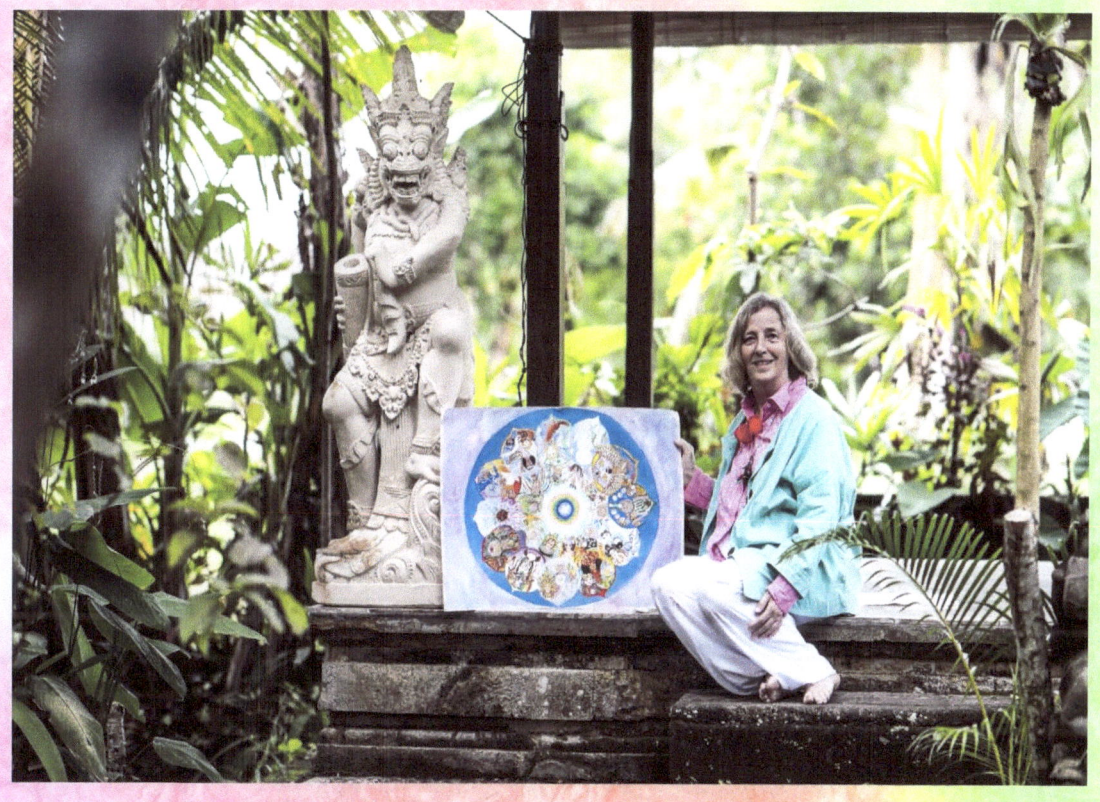

Della Burford with her Goddess painting painted in Leema Graham studio in 1995 in Toronto.

Dale Bertrand leading his Medicine Wheels workshop at the Spirit of Writing and Art in Bali. Below he is sharing his "Stone Book of Knowledge" which he produced with the writing of John Hugh Roberts from Wales.

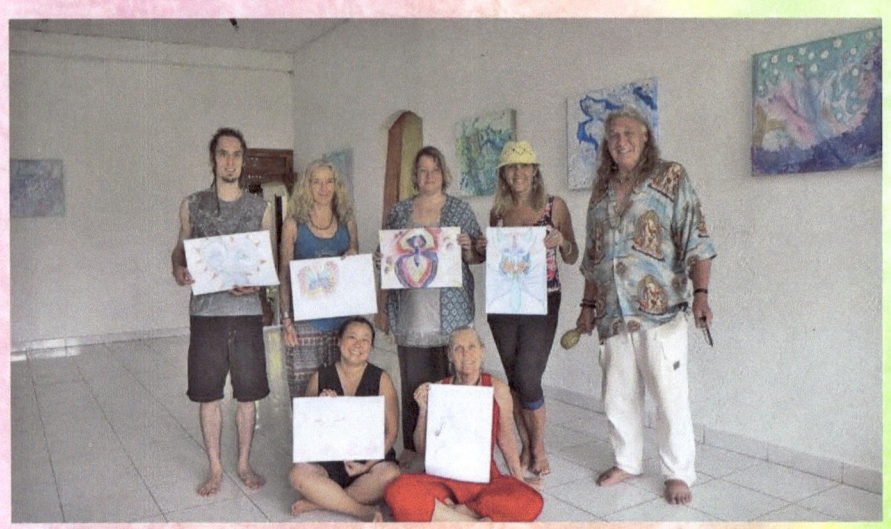

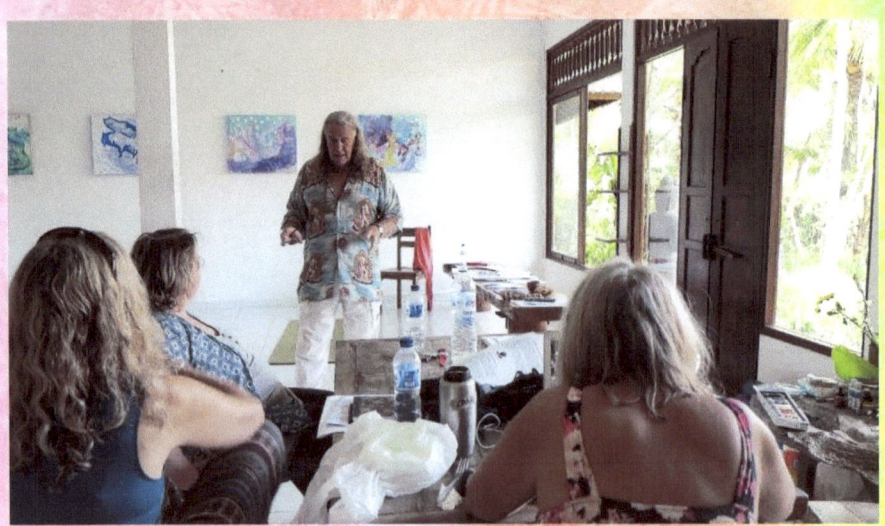

"Bali is one of the few cultures with origins in one of the great ancient cultures which is still alive." Arthur Erickson

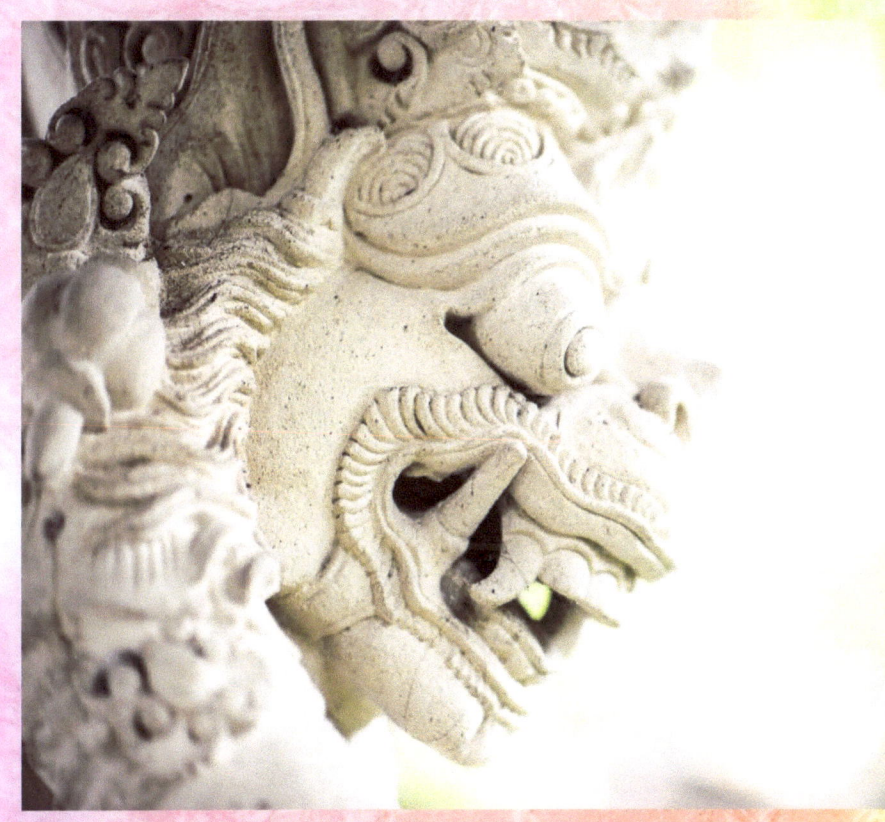

Statue found outside the studio we paint in at Spirit of Writing and Art.

"Do not dwell in the past, do not dream of the future, concentrate the mind on the present moment."
Buddha

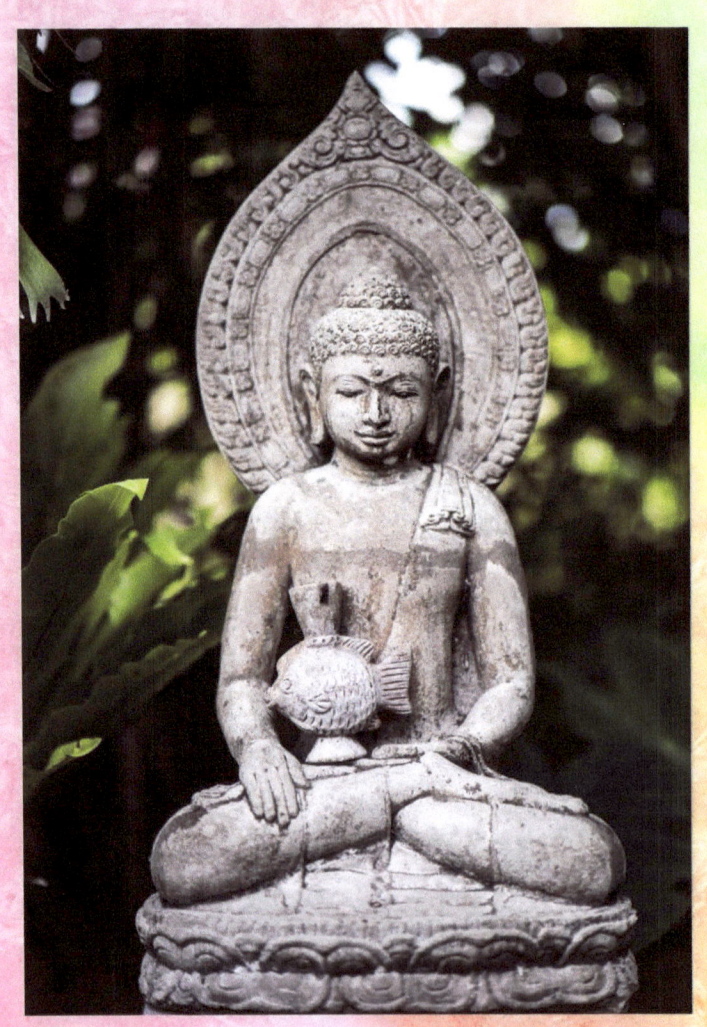

"There is nothing so stable as change."
Bob Dylan

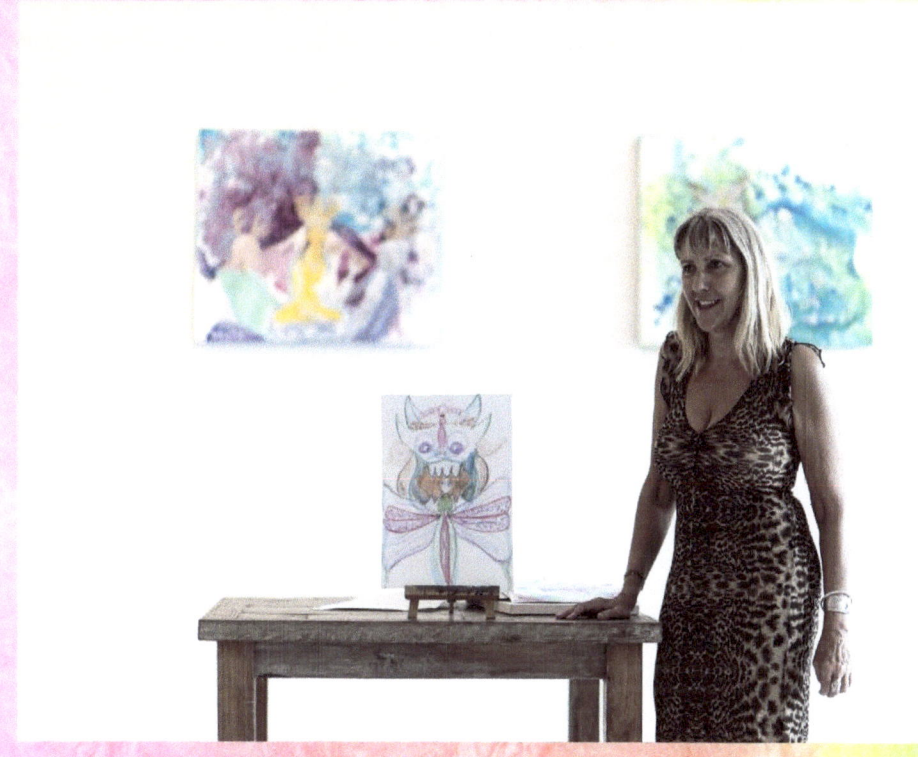

Charlyne Chiasson

"Music doesn't lie. If there is something to be changed in this world, then it can only happen through music." Jimi Hendrix

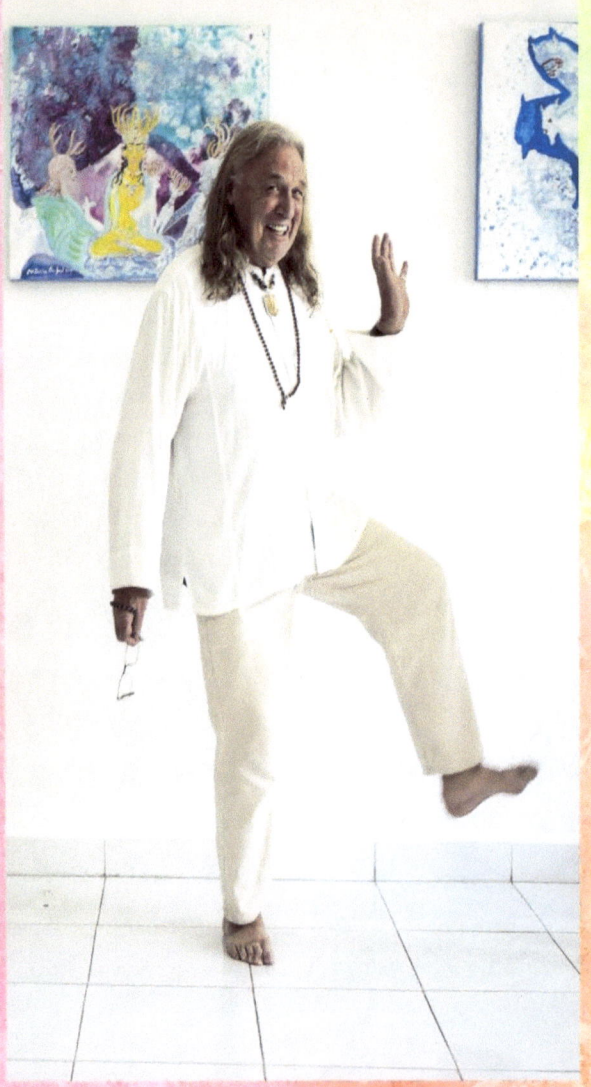

Dale Bertrand in Bali

"A friend is someone who gives you total freedom to be yourself." Jim Morrison

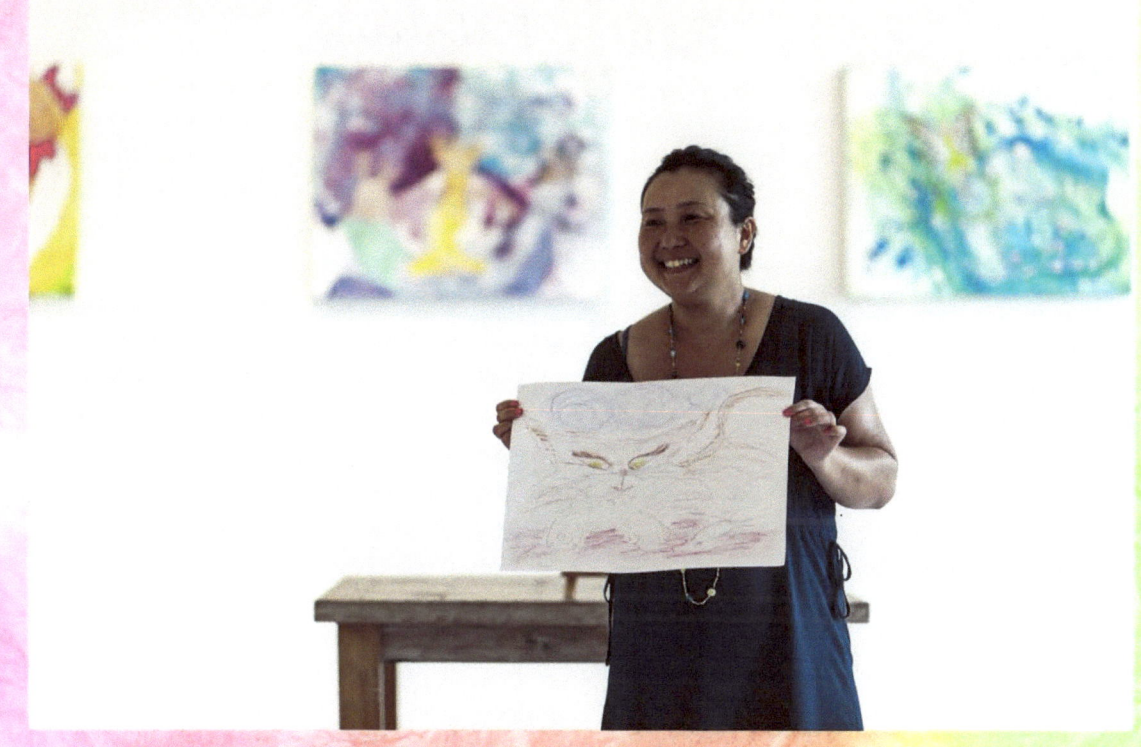

Grace Po with painting from workshop.

"I believe that imagination is stronger than knowledge. That myth is more potent than history. That dreams are more powerful than facts. That hope always triumphs over experience. That laughter is the only cure for grief. And I believe that love is stronger than death." Robert Fulghum

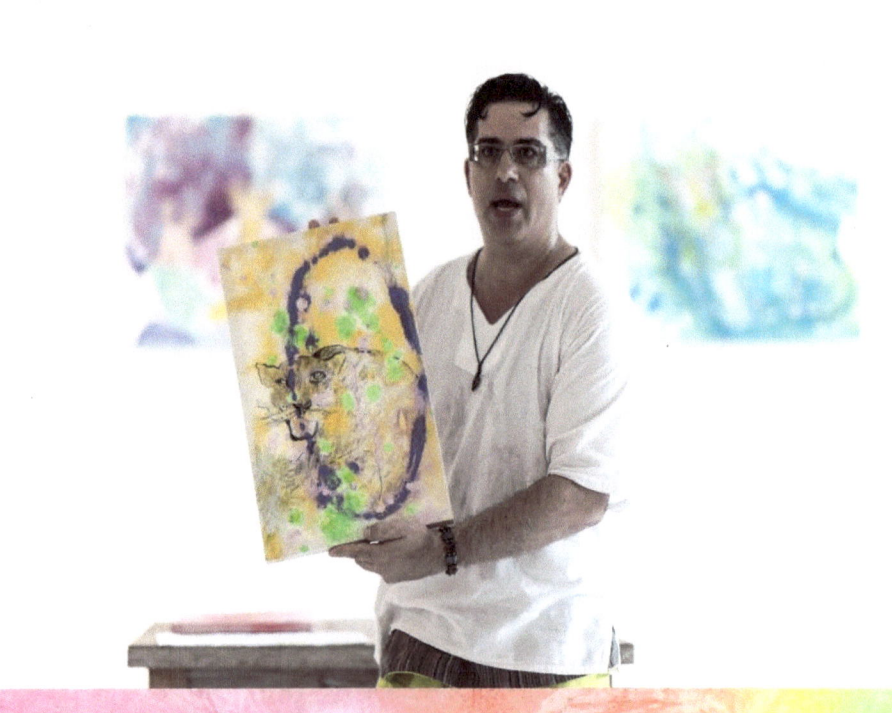

Wallace Murray

"The essence of pleasure is spontaneity."
Germaine Greer

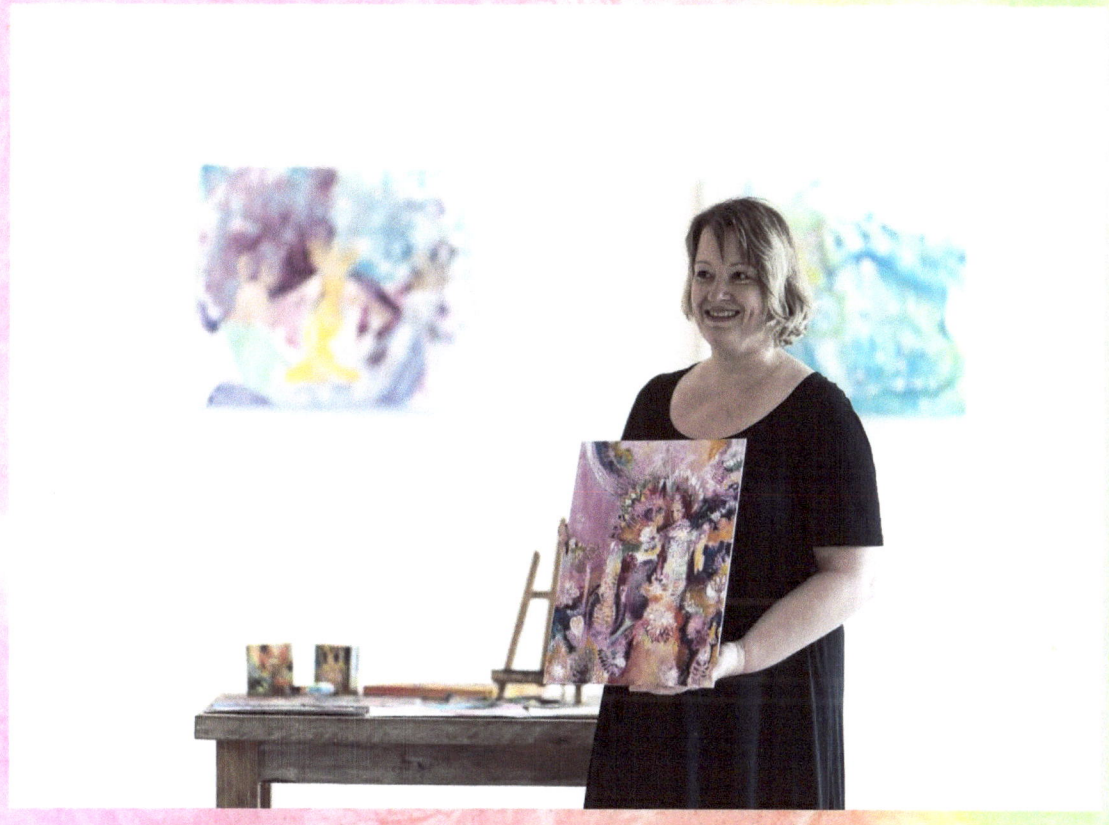

Sylke Gande with a painting done at the Spirit of Writing and Art in Bali. Sylke paints in a very spontaneous style. Sylke taught a class on Sacred Art.

"The best and most beautiful things in the world cannot be seen or even touched – they must be felt with the heart."
Helen Keller

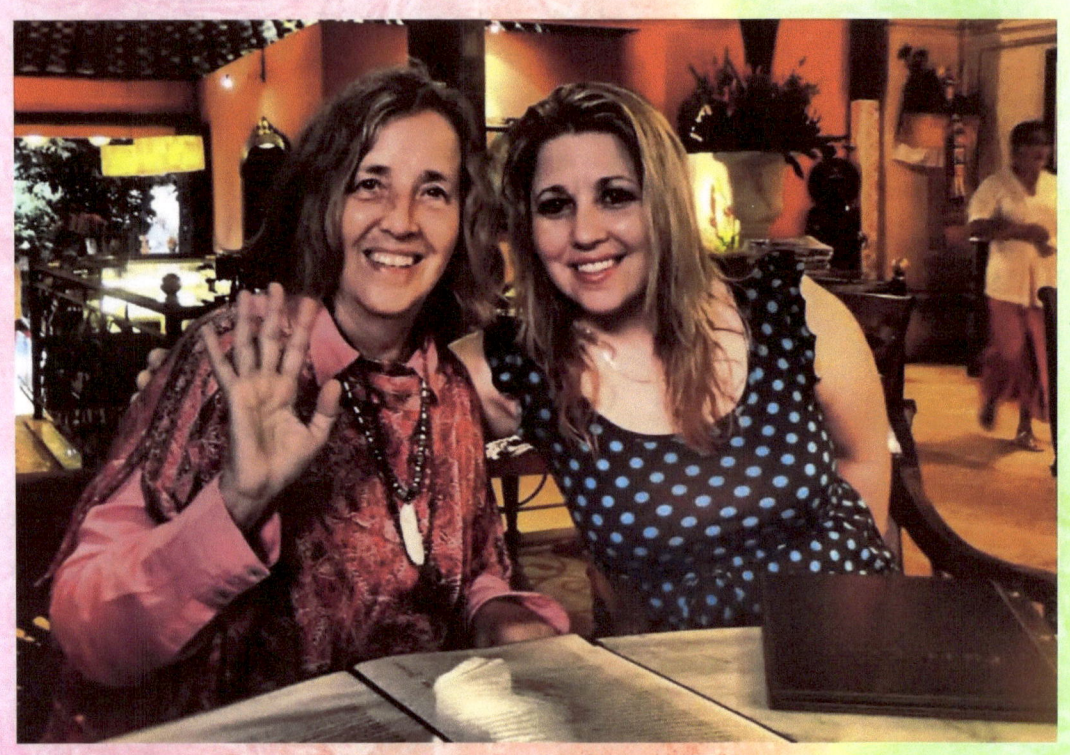

Della Burford with her neice Holly Yurxa in Bali at the Spirit of Writing and Art 2016.

"Happiness is when what you think, what you say, and what you do are in harmony." Mahatma Gandhi

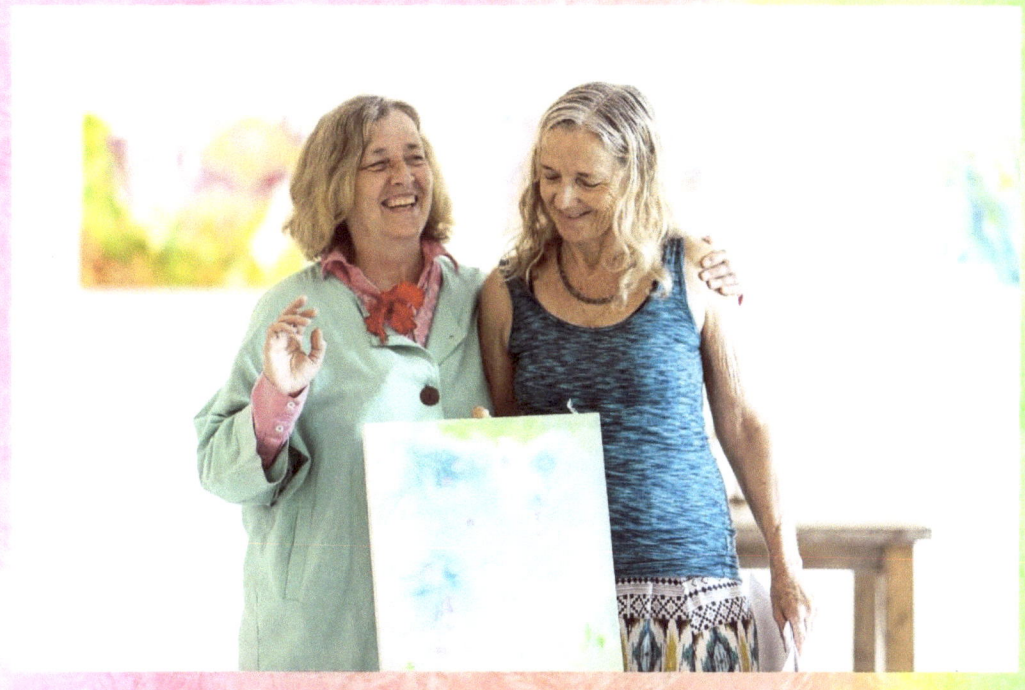

Della Burford and Norah Burford at Spirit of Writing and Art, Bali.

"A friend is what the heart needs all the time." Henry Van Dyke

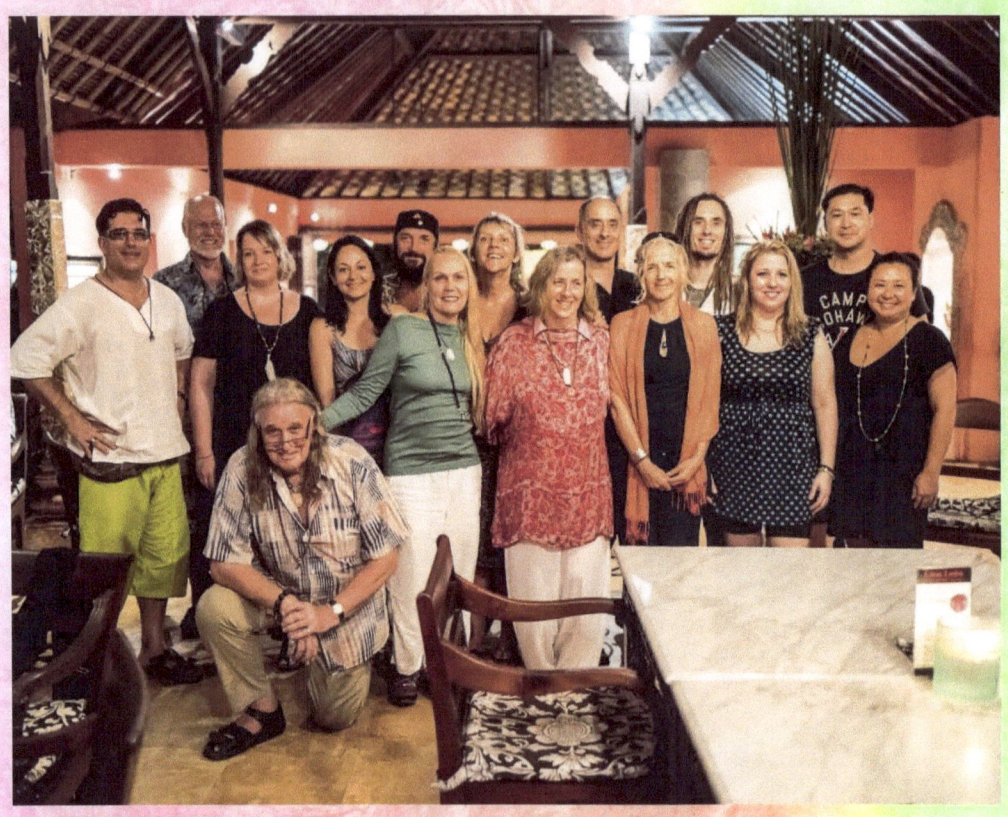

Final Feast at the Spirit of Writing and Art in Bali. Also was the big 70 birthday for Della Burford. hanks to all of those who came.. yes friendship is what the heart needs.

"The world is full of beauty; you are the greatest proof of this."
— Matshona Dhliwayo

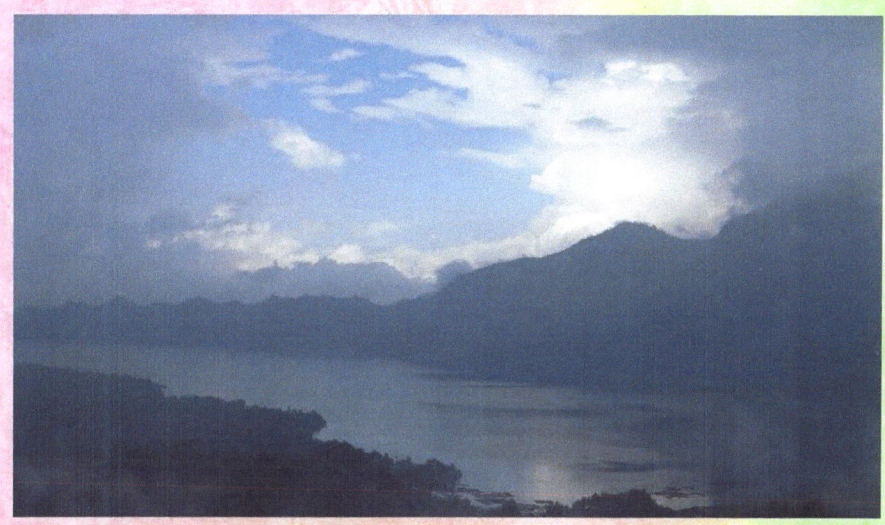

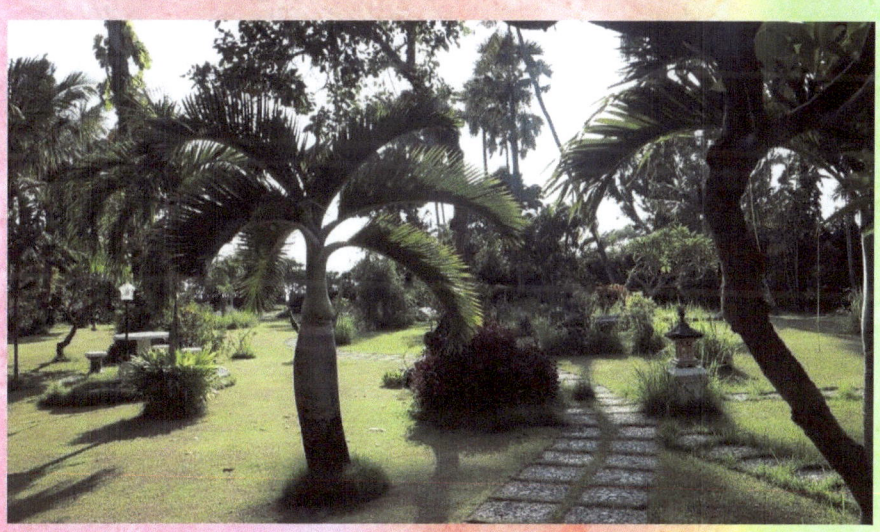

Lake Batur and Ahmed.

"Joy in looking and comprehending is nature's most beautiful gift." Albert Einstein
I felt this quote when at Christina Hatala's Villa Flamboyant in Ahmed. Ketut met us there and helped us in many ways.

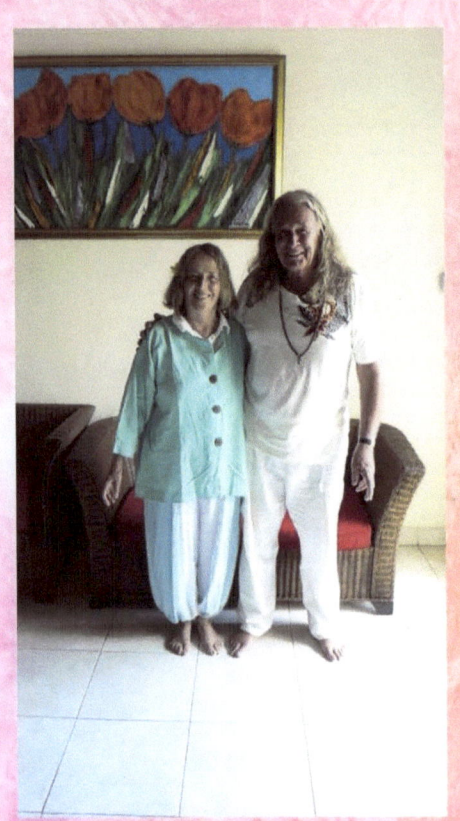
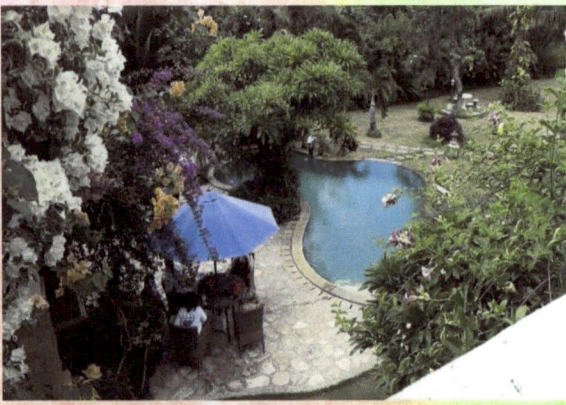
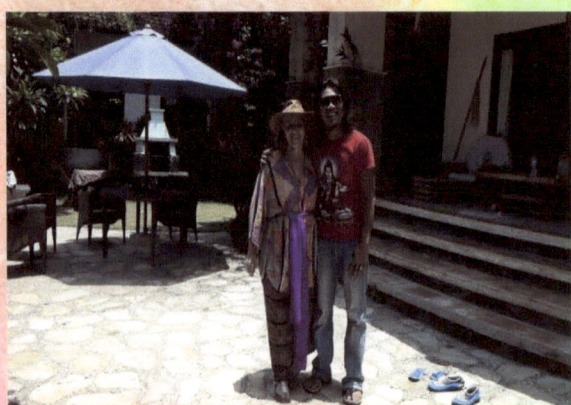

"Every great dream begins with a dreamer. Always remember, you have within you the strength, the patience, and the passion to reach for the stars to change the world."
Harriet Tubman

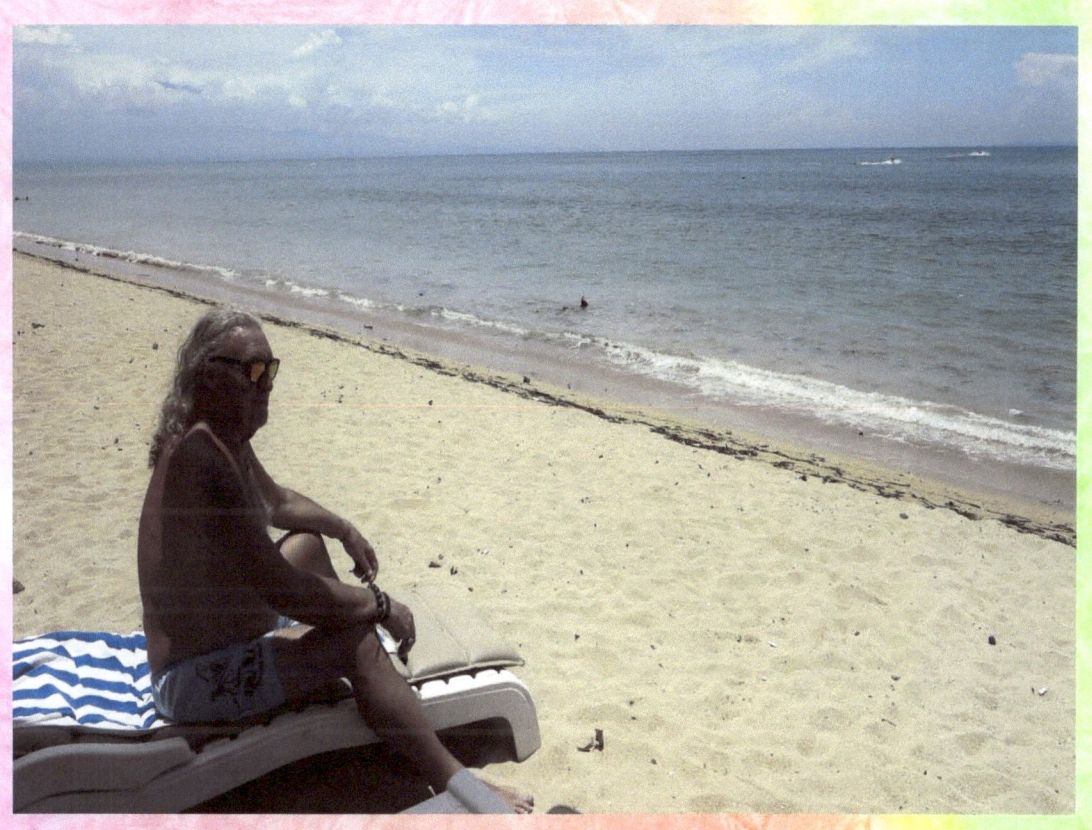

Enjoying the beach at Sanur in Bali... reflecting on the greater meaning of dreams.

"The good man is the friend of all living things." Mahatma Gandhi

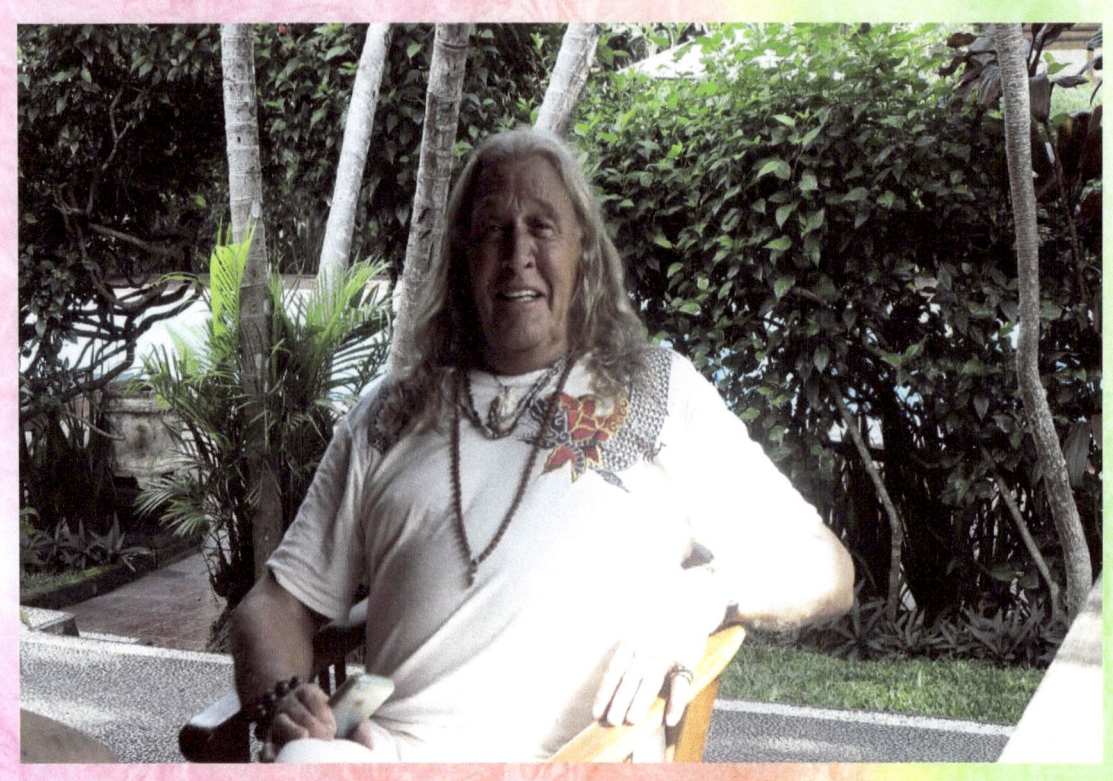

Dale Bertrand at the Spirit of Writing and Art in Bali.

I have found that if you love life, life will love you back. Arthur Rubinstein

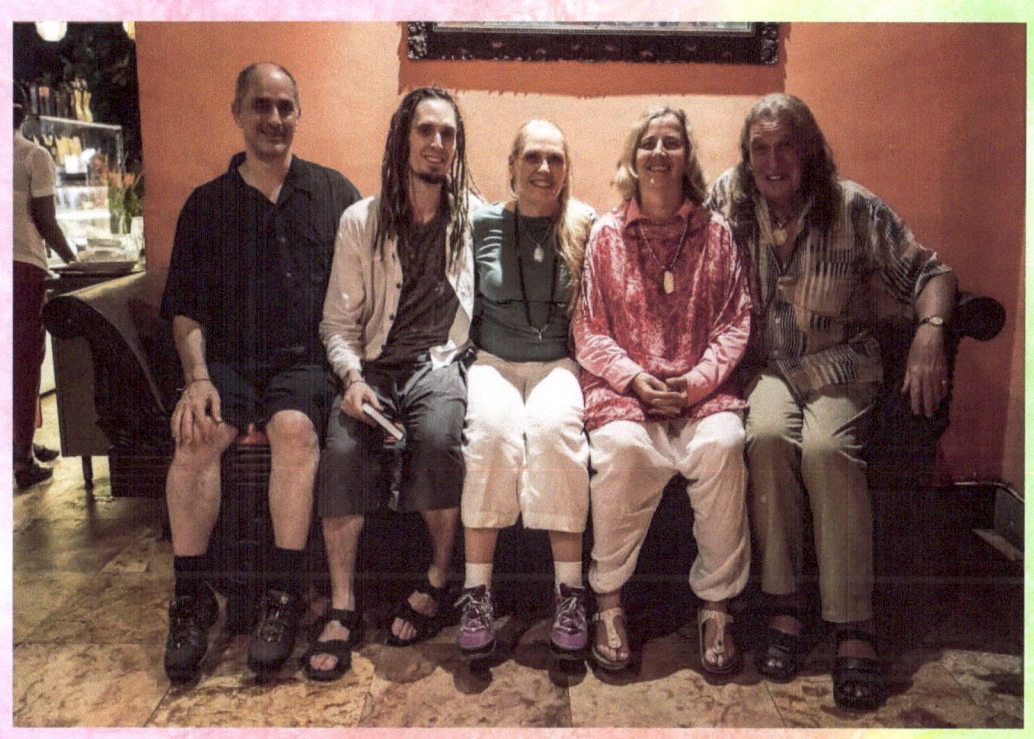

Dear friends with Della and Dale .. Leema Graham, Ayden Graham and Eric Bobrow from California. Here we felt like kids again as our feet didnt touch the floor.

Shared the "Dream Wheels" and "Dream Keys" story at Pelanghi school in Bali with the children. Dale also shared his Druid illuminated books. Thanks to Michelle Pettit and all staff at the school.

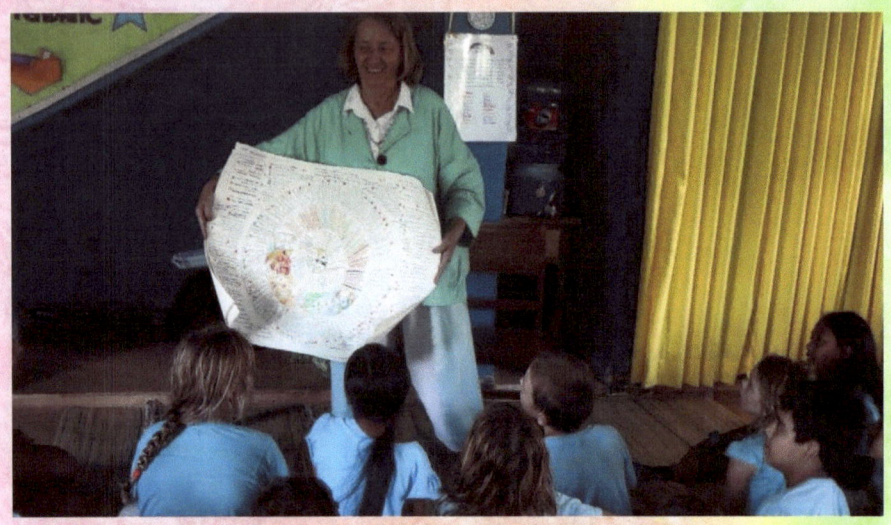

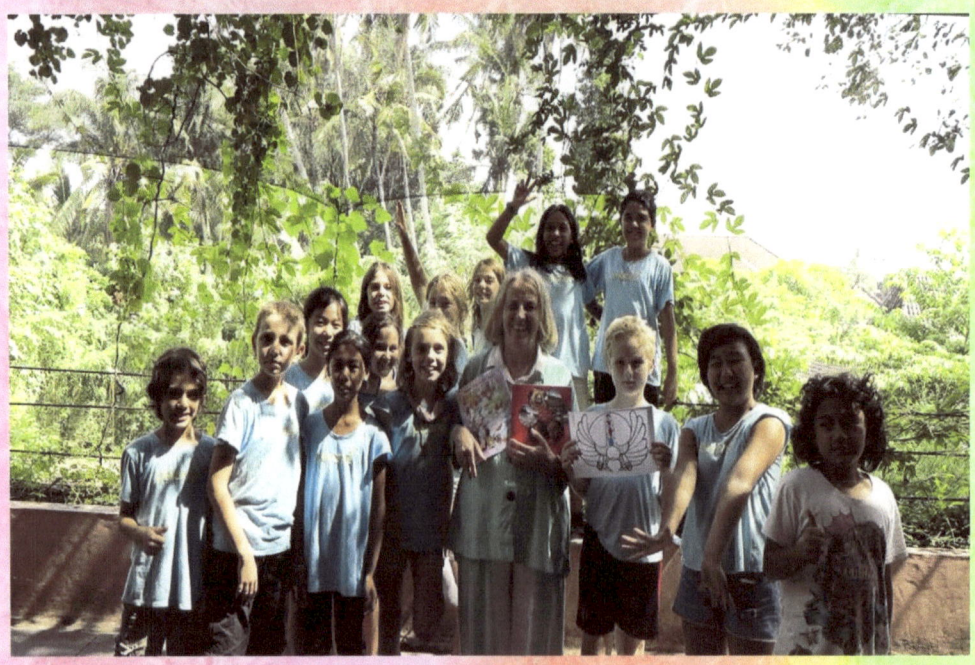

Our dream in 2017 will be this show of 30 artists at the Spirit of Writing and Art in Bali.

"Imagination Reigns" in Ubud Bali
at Spirit of Writing and Art - Jan 27th - Feb 5th 2017 Opening 27th 4-8
Hosted by Della Burford/Norah Burford & Dale Bertrand
Show of the Members of the "Society for Art of Imagination"

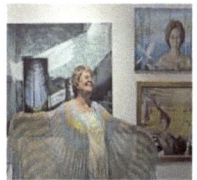 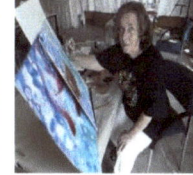 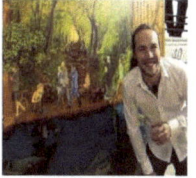 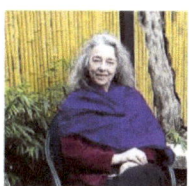

Brigid Marlin-Founder | Della Burford-Coord | Jean Pronovost | France Garrido

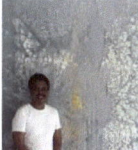 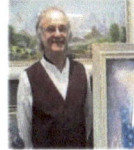 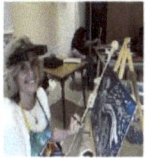 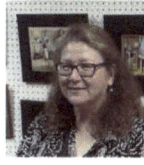 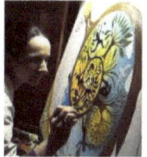 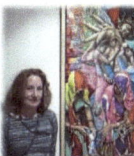

Wayan Karja Host in Bali | Benny Anderson | Cynthia Re Robbins | Debra Keirce | Gaia Orion | Kathleen Scarboro

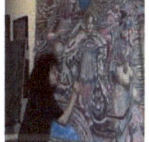 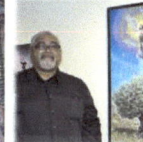 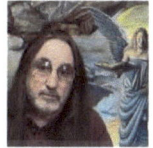 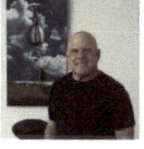 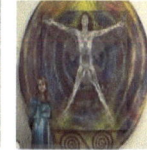 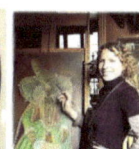

Olga Spiegel | Miguel Tio | Michael Coleman | William Otto | Irene Vincent | Liba W.S.

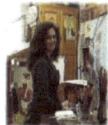 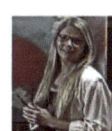 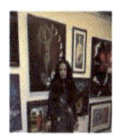 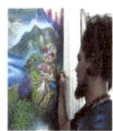 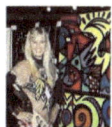 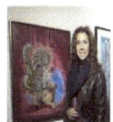 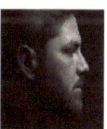

Lyne Lafontaine | Joanne St. Cyr | Rosemary Stehlik | Chris Dyer | Margot Bussiere | Heiidi Taillefer | Jerome Bertrand (former admid)

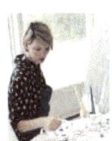 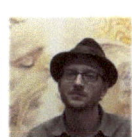 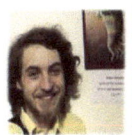 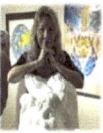 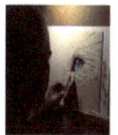 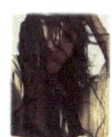 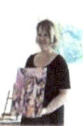

Georgina Smith | Dustyn Lucas | Ricky Schaede | Zeerka | Andrew Gonzalez | Fay Marineau | Sylke Gande

www.ingramcontent.com/pod-product-compliance
Lightning Source LLC
Chambersburg PA
CBHW051209220526
45473CB00003B/966